YOU HAVE BEEN
Catfished

Wanda Stevens Reilly

NEWMAN SPRINGS PUBLISHING
320 Broad Street
Red Bank, NJ 07701

First originally published by Newman Springs Publishing 2023

ISBN 979-8-88763-578-1 (Paperback)
ISBN 979-8-88763-714-3 (Digital)

Printed in the United States of America

To my sons—Johnny, Andrew, and George—and Susan Andrews for giving me a place to stay and finish my book.

Thank you, Hope, for letting me stay in your room.

Mom and Dad Curt and Shirley Stevens and my grandparents Grandma and Grandpa Stevens and Grandma and Grandpa Flood who are my angels in heaven.

To Mark thank you for believing in me, and being a great friend as well.

And to Wiliam Michael and Barbara Ann for being there for me. You are my family.

To my best friend, Tommy, and his wife, Paula. Thank you for always believing in me, and thank you for being the wonderful people that you are.

I also want to thank Dean Annette and Manchester, New Hampshire, for the car and taking us in. I will always be grateful to you.

Thank you, Eileen and Gary, for letting me stay at your home in New Hampshire when I came up to see my kids.

To all the other people who have touched my life and helped me along the way, you know who you are and what you mean to me. Thank you so much for all you have done for me on this journey. I truly appreciate every one of you. You have touched my heart, and you are my angels. Thank you so much.

March 8, 2018—today was a day of joy that, in the later months, would turn into hell on earth and the demise of my spirit. This may have been my karma in this lifetime or the last lifetime.

My name for this book will be Jenna. This is a real encounter, and this is how it started.

I was a medical coder at a prominent hospital in Manchester, New Hampshire. On my lunch hour, I checked my Facebook and saw a very handsome man in an army uniform that wanted to friend me.

In November of the past year, I had volunteered at the hospital, putting together a veterans care package program through the hospital where I worked. I was thinking, *Maybe this is one of the soldiers that is reaching out to me.* I friended him and waved to him, and we started talking in Messenger. He seemed very nice, not like some of the guys I have dated in the past—ugh.

I told him that I worked on a veterans care package and wanted to know if there was anything I could send over for the troops.

He told me his name was Eric. I won't say the last name, and I am not sure this was his name at all. But I am going to call him Eric for this book.

Eric said there was nothing I could send the troops, which should have been a red flag for me, but I didn't catch on. Eric did tell me that he was missing his son, Jerry, and that his birthday was on March 8. He said, "Because I am in Iraq and my son is in Ghana, Africa, I am not able to send him anything."

This should have been another red flag for me, but I was in a very vulnerable state and living in a place I did not want to live in. My heart went out to his plight. I then asked, "How can I help you?" And this is how it all started.

Eric told me that his son wanted a phone, and I said I didn't have that kind of money. I could only send him $60 but did not know how to get it to him. Eric then proceeded to let me know how I could send this money to him. He explained that I needed to go to a Western Union and to send it to his son's teacher, Whitney. His son would then get the money that Whitney would pick up.

I asked why his son was not with him, and he told me that where he was, was very dangerous and not safe for his son. I thought, *Okay, that is plausible*, so I sent $60 to Whitney through Western Union. This is how the money exchange began.

Western Union has a process, and they state right on there that if you do not know this person, to not send any money to them. Somewhere in my disconnected brain and my big heart, I chose to bypass this and told them that yes, I knew this man. (If you are in the same situation, please let the authorities know that you do not know the man you are sending money to.)

The soldier was so grateful that I had done this for him and his son that he sent me a song. That literally made me cry. The song was titled "Good Morning, Beautiful" by Westlife. I thanked him, and so it started.

When I first sat down to write this book, I tried to copy our conversations onto a Grammarly document. It worked for about three months of conversation, but the feed was too big to cut, copy, and paste onto a Grammarly page. Then I tried to transfer the conversation to a Word document, but I couldn't do that either. I am not computer savvy.

I am now sitting in a park, writing out my experience by hand. I am doing this for anyone who is going through a similar experience. I pray that if someone is beginning a relationship online and it is someone that the person has never met and does not know, then I pray you proceed with caution.

Ladies and gentlemen (yes, this goes for both genders), there are people in this world who will prey on the elderly, lonely, single, or married—anyone with a heart.

The term for this kind of behavior is *catfishing*. This is when a person posts a picture of a good-looking man or woman and pretends to be the person in the picture. The person will romance you, and they know how to make you love them or fall in love with them. Then they proceed to ask you for money. They may tell you that it is for their box—that has money and gold in it, or they may tell you it is for their sick son or sick teacher. They may tell you that they have been wounded in a war and need money to get out of there or that their son is going to get kicked out of school. It is always a different story, but the purpose is the same: to pull at your heartstrings and have you help them out. This is a ploy to get you to part with your hard-earned money so that they can do whatever they want with it.

I am not the only one this has happened to, and this goes on every single day. I am told they do this to at least fifty people at a time. I found out a little too late—after I had given all the money I had. Eric never ever intended to pay me back. I pray that this person who took my money really needed it.

What was told to me much later was that the person probably partied with it, bought drugs with it, was maybe sex trafficking, or last but not least, bought guns with it. This thoroughly turned my stomach.

I felt stupid, ashamed, and guilty for spending all my mutual funds, which I wanted to leave for my sons, on a romance scammer. I felt betrayed, disrespected, and just empty inside. I had plenty of friends that told me to watch out for army people posing as people who needed money, but my brain and heart wanted to believe that he was not like those others, that this man was different.

Every question I asked him, Eric had a plausible reply. He told me his name was Eric Q. I don't know if this was his real name or not. I believed what he said as the truth. Later I would find out that it was all a lie.

I wonder if the handsome man in the picture knew that he was part of a romance scam.

I could have had my own apartment by now. I could have paid on my car so that I wouldn't have it repossessed. I could have paid off my debt in the credit bureau. I could have a bank account now. But because I helped this man, I had to live with friends and family for the past year. I have moved four times and am now living out of my car while sleeping at my mother and father's house. Later I will move in with my cousins Susan and George as they had an extra bedroom. I thank the people who took me in on my journey, and I am truly grateful for the experiences that I had. But it has been a rough road.

I now belong to a romance scammer group. I will not mention their name because this is an anonymous group of people who have gone through the same thing that I have. I can let you know that if you do have someone that you think may be doing this to you, you can upload a photo of the man or woman to Socialcatfish.com. They will then let you know how many hits this person has had, if any. This person that you think you are talking to may not even know that his/her picture is being used for this kind of scam. You may be talking to someone totally different.

There are so many people losing their homes, cars, money, and respect because of their good hearts. These are the people who want to believe the best in someone and the good in people. We honor their word and believe that they will do what they promised us and that they will return our money.

These people will tell you that they will pay you back double; and when you stop paying the bill, they will tell you that if you paid just a little bit more, they would have been able to help you out. This is baloney. They have no intention of helping you ever, and they don't care what financial burden they put on you. It is all about them and how much they can get out of you.

The person that you are messaging will say exactly what you want to hear. He/she will let you know that you are the only person that they want to be with.

Eric and I talked for eight months before I caught on to what was actually happening. I was always questioning but accepted whatever he had to say because I believed in my heart that he would never take advantage of me. To top it all off, I had lost all my money, and the money was not coming in as it had been before because I had also changed careers that year. When my money dried up, Eric was starting to have other people send me money. This is was when I started really questioning what was going on. Why weren't these other people sending Whitney money? Why were they sending it to me and having me send it to Whitney? It didn't make any sense. I felt like a middleman.

I finally called a lawyer and found out that the term used for what was being done to me was *catfishing*, and this is what these scammers do.

I also found out that the term for what Eric wanted me to do was *money laundering*. I knew the word since I had studied the term in my insurance exam but did not know how it all worked. Now I do.

If your scammer sends you money and asks you to send it to another person, beware. This is money laundering. The lawyer I talked to then told me I should let the FBI know what was going on. I did do this, and I stopped sending him money. I did talk to an FBI agent and was told that this happens a lot and that I would probably never see my money again because the people that do this are in a different continent, and the FBI doesn't have jurisdiction in that country. I was devastated and felt like I had lost my best friend and my lover at the same time. The man I was talking to was not that man at all; it was someone totally different.

I thought, *Hell, I have read about money laundering*, but never knew how it worked. I was horrified that I could be doing something like this without even knowing. Please, if you are doing this now, stop and call a lawyer or the FBI. Do not send these people money anymore. Do not play their middleman game.

My whole world was crumbling, but I thought, *Okay, this is part of my karma and my payment for being so blinded to his deception.*

I started crying, and when I was talking to the FBI agent, she told me that unfortunately, they weren't able to find out who the person really was.

I will probably never see my money again. His romantic approach was very convincing. He was an expert in his line of business.

I am looking forward to my future positive karma.

I am going to write about key points for those of you going through this now. This book was written for those of you that lost money already, for those of you who have fallen in love with a false person, and for those of you who have been deceived by a scammer. This book is for those that have been berated by family and friends for the choices you have made. I pray for you. This is for those of you that have been preyed on. I am praying for you, and I pray that you find this book and read it. I hope that you heal from the devastation that has been brought into your life.

In hindsight, I think this happened to me so that I could stand in my light and tell you this story of those eight months of my life. I thought last night that maybe I needed to write this out because when I was fourteen, my mother and father read my diary. At the time, I had a lot of anger toward my mother. Writing in my diary was a way to get out my anger. My mother and I were not getting along, and when my father told me that they both read my diary, I felt violated.

I am all over this now, but the reason that I tell you this is because I have never written anything since—not my feelings, not anything. If I do, I burn it right away. This is the first time I stand in my truth. This is the first time that I write my feelings down on paper again since I was fourteen years old.

I took the diary and burned it in the woodstove. I have never written my feelings down again. I have forgiven both parents, but I have never forgotten the intrusion. This is a huge step for me to write my feelings down in a book.

I know some of you will read this and say, "What was she thinking? Why didn't she see this coming? Why did she give her money to this man?" I have asked myself the same questions. I don't believe there is an answer for them.

I am sure a psychologist or a psychiatrist would have a label for what I did, such as being an enabler or codependent. Whatever it is, I did it, and I take complete responsibility and ownership of my actions. I am starting with a clean slate now. I am aware of what these people do, and I am working to catch these people through Social Catfish so they can't do this to anyone else.

I am calling myself Jenna because I love the name. I was going to call my firstborn Jenna. But my firstborn was a boy, so no Jenna for me.

I am putting all my faith into this book, and I am feeling the fear of writing my thoughts and feelings onto paper once again as I did in my diary. There will be those who judge me, but this is my truth. This is what really happened to me, and I feel as though I need to write about it because there are so many people that are going through this right now.

If I can stop anyone from doing what I did by writing this book, this will have been worth it. I am feeling my fear and doing it anyway. Maybe the Holy Spirit, God, Jesus, angels, saints, guides, and the universe are helping me write again.

I don't know why this happened to me, but if I stay silent, if I don't speak my truth, then nothing will change. And this needs to be changed. We need to be aware of what these people are doing.

From the interviews I have watched of romance scammers on YouTube, they all seem to have no remorse or guilt about what they are doing.

I prayed and asked for strength to write this book, and I pray that I can help anyone in the US or other countries keep their money in their pockets and not give it to someone that doesn't deserve it.

I met him on March 8 on Facebook, and he wanted me to meet him on Hangouts (another app). After that, this is how it went.

On March 9, 2018, Eric wrote to me that he wanted me to have conversations with him on Hangouts. He said that he could not be on Facebook because the UN would not allow them to be on social media. Now, I know that the reason was probably that Facebook caught on to what he was trying to do. This is what the romance scammers do. They meet you on Facebook and get you onto Hangouts. I am not sure why they want the conversation in Hangouts.

I trust people wholly and completely, so I never once thought that he was lying. I even told him about the first guy that I fell in love with that lied to me and told me he was divorced for eight years when he was still married and his wife was pregnant with his baby?

Eric didn't care that I had already been lied to. He knew he had a sucker. I told him I did not want to be lied to, and he told me he would never do that. Seriously? He kept saying, "I will pay you double." I told Eric, "I don't want double. I just want the money I put into your box and for your child."

These romance scammers will ask you to go to Hangouts, LinkedIn, or Tinder (don't go to Tinder, though; it is a hookup site only).

I am not sure why they picked Hangouts, but here are the texts he sent me for eight months until I figured out what he was doing. I will never know who this was. Was it an enemy? Was it a random stranger? Was it a relative that I didn't speak to anymore? (I do have valid reasons for not speaking.) Was it an ex that hated me? Was it an ex that wanted revenge? Was it an ex that had a crazy partner that did this to me? I have made a few enemies in my lifetime but not intentionally. Was it a friend that I blocked because they disrespected me? Was it the stalker I had in the past that I tried to get a restraining order on and couldn't because he hadn't threatened me? These are questions that run through my mind as I am writing all of this down.

When I called the attorney and the FBI, the FBI told me that it is very hard to catch these people because most of them are out of the country, pretending to be a US citizen on a peace mission, or an army or navy man.

Maybe it is my karma for asking my ex for money to leave the marriage. I didn't ask for his pension. I gave him the house so my sons could stay in their own home.

He told me I didn't own shit; that he would get the house, the kids, and the dogs; and that I didn't have a job; and he told me he would fight me in court for everything. He made the money. I was a stay-at-home mom with a child with asthma whose breathing I was constantly monitoring and another son with behavioral problems. I tried to keep the family together for years. The day my husband (at the time) told me I didn't own shit was the "aha" moment.

The next day, I went and put myself in school. I signed myself up for courses at Manchester Technical College. I haven't had the best luck with relationships, and yes, it does take two to tango. I am not innocent, but I don't think I deserved all that has gone on in my life either.

Now I am telling myself another story like Abraham Hicks says to do. I have always said that I picked the wrong guy. Now I am saying, "I have a wonderful man that treats me as if I am the only one he has ever wanted." Instead of me saying, "Why do I always pick the men that have someone else in their life?" I am saying, "I pick a man that has been looking for his one woman, a man that doesn't have anyone in their life, and a man that doesn't want anyone but me. This man is strong, muscular, intelligent, and kind, and he loves animals and children but doesn't want any more children. This man is a man that wants to travel, spend time in nature, and wants to dance or wants to watch me while I dance. A man that likes to sing and to meet people."

I was reading *The Power of Your Subconscious Mind*, by James Murphy, when this army man came into my life; and I was in a very vulnerable state for three years. I planned to get out of a situation that I had been in, and each time I was ready to leave, something else would happen. However, I kept telling my subconscious mind that I would get out of this situation.

I am now single, not in a relationship. No one has said that they wanted to be in a relationship exclusively. The closest I have gotten to that happening is a Florida friend that told me that he was in a relationship with me, and I questioned him, "We are in a relationship?" He sent me a GIF on Facebook saying, "Is this relationship making you miserable?"

What part of the man's brain disconnects when he starts to have feelings?

So now I say, "My man does not have anyone in his life that he is seeing, and he is truly faithful, loving, and kind toward me."

I am no longer self-sabotaging myself. I know my worth, and I no longer am going to be sucked into a game of manipulation.

Here is my truth and my story of what really happened to me last year. I did not tell anyone for a very long, long time. I was humiliated and embarrassed of what I did. I am now letting everyone know what happened because I want to help all of you or your friends who may be in the same situation that I was in. Pay attention to the conversations below.

March 8, 2018

Eric: Let's chat on Hangouts.

Jenna: Hi, I am in finally.

Eric: Wow, cool, I know you're more intelligent than you think, dear. I want us to chat here, okay?

Eric: I will be signing off Facebook so I won't be blocked by the UN. If I am on social media while still on a mission, they are going to block my page. So I want us to have conversations on here, okay?

Jenna: Okay.

Eric: So what are you doing at the moment?

Jenna: Still coding cardiology.

Eric: Okay, text me when you are free. I will reply if I am still awake.

Jenna: Okay, get some sleep. I don't want to keep you up all night.

Eric: I am always at your service, madam. LOL. I will text you when I wake up. I don't sleep for long. Take care of yourself, dear.

Jenna: Okay.

March 10, 2018

Jenna: It is 5:17 p.m. What time is it there? I hope I didn't wake you up.

Eric: I am here now, my dear. How is work going today? I haven't slept yet. I have been doing some paperwork, but I am through with it now. The time here is 4:40 a.m., and I have to rest for a short while. Good night. Sweet dreams. I will talk to you soon.

Jenna: Sweet dreams, Eric.

Eric: I wish I could be beside you as you open your cute eyes. I would brush my fingers by your hair and lay your hands aside, then I would say a prayer for today to protect you from falling. Lastly, I would take your hands in mine and wish you a good morning.

Eric sent a good-morning picture with coffee.

Eric: With every morning is a new beginning. Always make your day a great one because it is God's gift for a new beginning, blessing, and hope. Good morning, dear. How was your night? I hope you slept well. Eric then sent the songs "True Colors" by Phil Collins and "It Hurts So Bad I Can't Take It Any Longer" by Westlife.

March 11, 2018

Jenna: Hi, Eric. I fell asleep. It is 3:45 a.m. here. Did you sleep well? Thank you for the wake-up songs. Every day is wonderful with you in it.

Jenna sent 209 and 210 from *The Power of Your Subconscious Mind.*

Eric: You are welcome. I am going to read this every day. Now go back to sleep and rest very well, okay, dear?

Jenna: I have been reading *The Power of your Subconscious Mind* and have been asking for someone like you to come into my life.

Eric: Wow, that sounds sweet to me, dear. God bless you so much, and I thank God for the first day I met you. I am going on patrol right now. I will text you when I get back to camp. Sleep tight, dear. 😊 💗

Jenna: Be safe. 😔 😊 [This was sent at 4:04 a.m.]

Eric: Hello, dear. I'm back from patrol. How are you doing, dear? I miss talking to you. I am thinking so much about you. Text me when you are free.

Jenna: Hi. Yes, I am free, and I can see your messages, yeah!

Eric: Okay, nice, so how is your day going today?

Jenna: I thought about you until I went to sleep. I kept pinching myself to see if this is just a dream.

Eric: LOL. It's not a dream, dear, okay? I feel the same way you do. And I feel blessed to have you in my life, dear.

Jenna: So what nationality are you? I have never heard of your last name before. Where did you come from? I saw your face and that smile. I don't know what it was, but it's like I knew you.

Eric: I am partly Mexican. My dad was from Mexico, but we lived in the States all our lives. I was born and raised in Orlando, Florida. What about you?

Jenna: My mother will tell you that we are 100 percent English, but I don't buy it. I think my grandfather was right. A little English, Irish, Scottish, Native American, and French. In other words, a mutt. LOL. I love your look.

Eric: Wow, cool, thank you so much, dear. Is it okay if I call you baby?

Jenna: You can call me anything except for swear words. 😆😆😆

Eric: My dear, at first I didn't believe, but I finally have this funny feeling in my heart for you. Now I believe what I feel for you is true, and no one that I have found will I forever love, respect, and cherish for all of my life, baby, except you. I promise to make you the happiest woman on earth, baby. You hold the key to my heart, and please don't hurt my feelings, baby.

Jenna: It is not in my nature to hurt anyone. I finally found you.

Eric: Wow, that is cool, baby. So what are your plans today?

Jenna: I plan to go to Dr. K's. It is a part-time job with not too many hours, but he is retiring soon. So I am helping them out with their ICD 10 codes. It is 12:00 p.m.

Eric: That is nice, and good afternoon to you, baby. The time here is 8:36 p.m., and I am going to have a word with the soldiers, okay, baby? I will text you when I get back.

Jenna: Okay, babe.

Eric: It won't take long, okay, sweetie? Kisses and hugs to you, baby. 

On Friday morning, she sent the song "Africa" by Toto to Eric. She let Eric know that every Friday morning, Rock 101 in Manchester, New Hampshire, played "Africa" by Toto and that she sang along to it every Friday.

Eric: Wow, baby. I love the song, and I love the picture. I will be
    looking at it every minute. How was your day today?
Jenna: I was just leaving in a little bit. I did some laundry before.
Eric: Baby, you should have called me. I would have helped you with
    the laundry.
Jenna: I am waiting for the laundry to dry before I go, ugh. Somehow
    I can't see you helping me with the laundry. What time is it?
Eric: It is 11:51 p.m., baby.
Jenna: Okay, you must be so tired. I am listening to the song you sent
    me today. I have goosebumps.
Eric: Wow, that is good to hear. Babe, have you eaten?
Jenna: I had an English muffin with peanut butter. Have you eaten?
Eric: No, baby, I do not eat at night so I don't sleep for long.
Jenna: Oh, then do you eat in the morning?
Eric: Oh yes, I do eat every morning.

* * * * *

As long as I was sending Eric money, I was his honey, his baby,
his love, and his queen; and he even called me his wife. I mirrored
the same sentiments to him. I loved him with all my heart. I thought
I found the one who would never ever hurt me, but alas, it was all a
facade.

In my heart, I believed he wanted me the way I wanted him.
I believed in the dream. I was so wrong; he never wanted me that
way. He wanted whatever money I came into or had. It was all his.
I would get paid, and he would butter me up really nicely. As I am
reading and writing this, I can't believe that I fell for this. I can see
now that he really wasn't very sincere, especially at the end when he
was getting mad because I wasn't making as much as I did.

* * * * *

Jenna sent Eric a Rascal Flatts song and asked if he ate in the
afternoon. She was worried about him eating and getting enough rest
because he was in Iraq, fighting the war.

Eric: Not all the time, baby. I love the song you sent.

Jenna: I have been trying to find the perfect song for you. This one hit a chord in me.

Eric: I love you so much, baby.

Jenna: I love the song you sent me. It made me cry good tears.

Eric: Wow, I am glad you love it, honey. I need you and love you and will do so for the rest of my life.

Jenna: I love the song, and I love the way you let me know exactly what you are feeling. I hear you loud and clear, and I believe you see in your heart that I feel the same way as you. As silly as that sounds, we have never met, but there is a definite connection. I don't know how that happens, but I am going to go with it.

Ever since I experienced this and this connection, I have had a much stronger connection with a couple of men that I have dated. The connection was even stronger than this fake connection, and they were real men that I had feelings for. None of the relationships have come to fruition. I am still in the "in between" mode. One day, this will happen for me once I get my finances in order again; but for now, I will keep writing this. And I pray that it will help some of you.

Jenna: Do you like to kiss? I have strong feelings for you.

Eric: Wow, that touched my heart so much, baby. I love you so much more, baby. Oh yes, I love kissing so much.

Jenna: I love a powerful kiss, not a peck on the lips like you give your grandmother. I like a kiss that is a "kiss me like a man means it" kiss. I have only been kissed like that once, and I knew the man on and off for eight years. He never once told me he loved me. I had to let him go because the relationship was one-sided only.

Jenna: Ever since this time, I have had two more men that kissed me like they meant it. Although it did not work out with them, I will never forget the kiss.

Eric: Wow, cool, I really love a hard kiss, one that will stop your breathing for a few minutes.

Jenna: Mmmm, I want a kiss that will make you weak in the knees.

Eric: Do you like when a man sucks you?

Jenna: Tongues touching, not slurpy, for the kiss but also electricity shooting throughout the body. The sucking depends on where. If you are talking about the cheek, then no. If you are talking about the breast, then hell yea! 😄

Eric: Oh yes, my favorite part is the breast. How long do you want your man to last in bed?

Jenna: It depends on how long we have. If we have all night, then for as long as we last. Then we lie in each other's arms and go to sleep.

Eric: Yes, that is it, baby. I love that. What are you doing at the moment?

Jenna: I am sitting in the living room, waiting for clothes to dry, so I can't put my load in. Sounds romantic, huh? It is almost five now. Time is flying.

Eric: Oh yes, the time is 1:23 a.m., and I am a little bit dizzy now, baby. I guess I have to rest for a short while. But I'm going to kiss you so much. I pray and dream about you. If I don't, I am going to wake up and go back to sleep again until I do dream about you.

Jenna: LOL. You are so funny. I just saw what you wrote. I am driving to work now. It is almost 5:30 p.m. I can't believe it. Sweet dreams to you.

Eric: Thank you, baby. Drive safely. I will text you when I wake up. I love you so much, baby. 💋💋💗

Eric then sent the song lyrics "I will be here, don't you cry."

Eric: You will be in my heart forever.

Jenna: I went to look at your profile on Facebook, and you are not on there anymore. Your pictures are gone. I hope you are sleeping well and that you are okay. I will dream of you tonight.

March 12, 2018

Eric: Say goodbye to the stars and the night, let the moon pass away, welcome the bright sunshine, let the rays of the sun brighten you up all over, and enjoy your morning, baby.

Eric: Sharing a smile is the easiest way to get your day started off right. Here is a smile so you can have a wonderful day today. Good morning, honey.

Eric: Baby, I am trying to log in to my Facebook account, and I have been hacked. How was your night? I hope you slept well. I wish you a wonderful day today. I am going to send you my pictures here on Hangouts. I can't access my Facebook account anymore.

Jenna: Oh, I hope I didn't wake you up. Who would hack your Facebook?

Eric: Baby, I don't know. I think the UN found out I am chatting with someone on social media.

Jenna: I went to sleep, then woke up thinking of you. It is 2:30 a.m. I am glad you are okay. I don't want you to get into trouble.

Eric: Oh, baby. There will be no trouble, honey.

Eric then sent Jenna four pictures of him, or the man that Jenna thought she was talking to, and one picture was of him and his dog.

Jenna: Oh my god, I love your dog. What is his name?

Eric: His name is Bully. LOL. what are you doing at the moment? Are you still in bed?

Jenna: Yes, I am. How about you? [Jenna did not tell Eric that she had been sleeping on a recliner for years.]

Eric: Oh, that is nice. I am going out, baby. I will text you when I get back to camp.

Jenna: Okay, I am going to try and get more sleep, but I will be up soon. I have to say your pictures look familiar. Have we met before? It is weird. I am not sure how your profile showed up in my Messenger.

Eric: I'm in my resting room, thinking about you, baby. Try to eat something. Baby, if work is gonna be stressful today, then call on me. And I will be there to help you, okay, honey?

Jenna: You are one of a kind. [Notice how Eric never answered Jenna's text about him looking familiar. Jenna never asked again because he was being romantic. She forgot all about what she had asked.]

Eric: Thank you, baby. That made me smile and my heart skip a beat.

Jenna: You are welcome. 😗 😗 😗

Eric: Hello, baby. How are you doing today, and how is work?

Jenna: Hello. Another snowstorm tomorrow. UGH! I will be working late tonight. How about you? How are you doing?

Eric: I am good, just that am missing you so much, baby.

Jenna: Awww, what time is it there?

Eric: The time is 12:00 a.m., baby. I believe you are so busy at the moment. I will always love you.

Jenna: I know you can't talk right now. Have a good day today.

Jenna: Was that "I will always love you," or was that a goodbye? LOL. Either way, what a way to go. LOL.

Eric: Hello, baby, I am back. Baby, it means I will love you forever. Honey, I am never going to say goodbye to a woman that holds the key to my heart, okay, baby?

Jenna: Awww, you are so awesome.

Eric: Thank you. Baby, what are you doing at the moment?

Jenna: I am starting work.

Eric: Baby, I will text you in the morning. I love you so much, honey. Kisses and hugs to my sweet baby.

Jenna: Hi, I am still at work. We went over another audit and had a meeting for Wednesday for the AAPC. I'm running on fumes. What time is it there? Sweet dreams to you. It is 8:00 p.m. here, and I am still at work.

Jenna: It's 11:05 p.m. I am still thinking of you while you are sleeping, hoping and wishing we could meet to hear your voice, see you smile, and hold your hand in mine for the very first time. I want to walk on the beach with you, our toes in the sand our, our bodies sweating and shimmering under the sun, and our hands intertwined together as one as we're talking, laughing, telling each other our innermost thoughts and feelings. We are able to tell each other anything good or bad without judgement. We listen and maybe give each other advice. We love and we share each and every aspect of our souls together, meshed into one sleep, my darling. Know that while you were sleeping, I asked and angels to look after you today, tomorrow, and until we meet Please, God, keep Eric safe from harm. Thank you, God, for watching out for this man while we get to know each other.

Eric: Wow, those are the sweetest words I've ever heard for so many years now, baby. I love you so much with no doubt. [Four days later, he was expressing his undying love for Jenna, and this is something that they do to make you trust them.]

Eric: My heart skips a beat whenever I see your message. My whole body needs you, baby. I want to be the man who will bring you coffee in bed every morning and the man who kisses you good night before we sleep at night. I want to kneel down and pray to God for giving me this special gift, and that is you, my love. I want to travel on vacation with you to any country of your choice, honey. Your thought is all over me. I can't wait to spend the rest of my life with you, honey. I wanna grow old with you, honey. I want to build a family with you, and I want to use the opportunity to say good morning to you, my heartbeat. Thinking of you gives me the greatest joy and happiness ever known, honey. How was your night? I hope you slept well, I love you so much. All my life, I've prayed for someone like you, honey. I wish you a wonderful day.

Eric sent two songs.

Jenna: My wish for you is that you will be safe today. Thank you for the songs, love. They were perfect. Thank you for making my morning so special. Yes, I feel the same way. I don't know how or why. But I am thanking God for bringing you into my life. [Later, Jenna would be cursing the devil for bringing him into her life.] I can't wait to meet you in person, but for now, I will cherish every text, every song, and all the beautiful words that you give me as a gift.

* * * * *

Yes, they were beautiful words. But did they come from him, or did he take them from other people who were writing to him? This is something I ask myself every day. It really doesn't matter. It was all fake, and he had no intention of ever meeting me.

* * * * *

Eric: Wow, baby, that is nice. I am back at camp now, honey. I came late today because things were so rough out there. I miss you so much.

Jenna: I am so sorry things are rough.

Eric: It is okay, baby. How are you doing today?

Jenna: Okay. I wish I were at work.

Eric: Baby, is there no work today?

Jenna: I took the day off because of the blizzard. But everyone who is home is someone I don't want to be living with, so it makes it difficult to have free space. It is okay. It is what it is. But by reading *The Power of Your Subconscious Mind*, which I got, I hope it will give me some ideas on how to make some money. Also, before I met you, I applied to a company for a remote coding position, and I think I am a strong candidate. When I get my own place, I can code from home.

Eric: So tell me, how are you preparing yourself to get a new apartment? [This is how they get you to tell them how much money you have and where you have it.]

Jenna: I have a small nest egg started. It has been difficult with all the bills. [Bingo. He thought she had a small nest egg for herself that she would not be using for an apartment.]

Eric: Oh, that is nice, baby. Have you eaten?

Jenna: Just an English muffin. How about you?

Eric: Not yet, baby. I will text you back shortly.

Jenna: Okay. It is 12:32 here. What time is it there?

Eric: The time is 9:03 p.m., and I will be back, okay, honey?

March 13, 2018

Jenna: It's 1:50 p.m. I know you are not there right now. I just wanted you to know that I wear a diamond on my right finger. It is my grandmother's ring. It is priceless to me. There are fifty-five years of marriage in this ring. She passed away in 1986, and my grandfather passed away in 1988. This is just in case you see it in a photo. It is eighteen-karat white gold. I don't like yellow gold. I loved my grandparents so much.

Eric: Wow, that is nice, baby. [At this point, he knew Jenna had a nest egg for an apartment and a ring that was worth some money.]

Eric: I am here now, my love. I miss you so very much. I have been thinking about you every second of my life. I love you so much. You really don't know how special you are to me. Baby, you are all I want in this life to make me happy for the rest of my life. [At this point, Eric knew just where to pull on Jenna's heart-strings, and he has probably had this conversation with many other women in the past or on the same day.]

Eric: Baby, can you send me a picture of the ring?

Jenna: "Yeah, and I uploaded the picture of my ring. [Don't tell them what kind of jewelry you have—ever.]

Eric: "Wow, that is lovely, honey. I am going to buy you a very lovely one for our wedding. Baby, that is a lovely hand. Okay, baby? [Five days in, and he was talking about their wedding and getting engaged.]

Jenna: You make me smile.

Eric: Baby, I vow that I will always make you smile and happy, and I am glad I am doing it now.

Jenna: ☺

Eric: Babe, I have something that's been troubling me since last night [Here it comes. Don't fall for this. He knew she had a nest egg and a ring that was priceless to her.] I don't know how to put it because I am ashamed of myself. Are you here with me? [At this point, he was going to try to get money out of Jenna.]

Jenna: What happened? I am here.

Eric: I received a message from our son last night about his school accommodation fee. Right now you know I am not around, and there is nothing I can do about it due to my job. They said they will give him a few days for his accommodation and his electric bill, or he will be thrown out. 😰😰😰😰😰

Jenna: Oh my god?

Eric: Honestly I don't know what to do or who to turn to, babe. It hurts me badly right now. I have not eaten since I received the message.

Jenna: How much does he need?

Eric: The fee is 500, and the electricity bill is 250. That's a total of 750.

Jenna: Yikes. How many American dollars? [If you send American money to Ghana, they get a lot more money than what you send.]

Jenna: I wouldn't have that much money to give. When does he need it? What day?

Eric: This week it runs out, babe. If you can do this for me, I promise to pay you back in double.

Jenna: Sweetheart, I can't get that much together by the end of the week. The money I saved is in an investment account. [Bingo. He knew she had an investment account.] If I had it available, I would give it to you.

Jenna: Won't you get paid soon? Can't they take it out of your check?

Eric: I swear on my honor, babe. [These scammers have no honor.]

Jenna: I don't get paid until next week. [Bingo. Now he knew she was getting a paycheck next week. He knew what day she got paid. And five days into it, he was calling his son *their* son. He knew a lot about Jenna, but Jenna didn't know a lot about Eric. And she didn't know what was really going on.]

Eric: I don't know if we could talk to them and see if they will wait until next week. [Sure, they could wait. It was Eric making up a story to extort money from Jenna.]

Jenna: I need to make a car payment, so even with my check, I don't know how much it would be. I am not sure I can come up with the whole thing. Is he still in Africa? If so, a little money goes a long way.

Eric: Babe, he said if the payment is not made, he will be out of his accommodations. Yes, babe, you are going to send it to the address you sent to him before when you sent him the $60. 😢😢😢

Jenna: I am sorry I can't help you until next week. I don't even have $60 right now. I don't know how much I will have next week. I am already planning to send something to this poor boy and his father, who is distraught. [At this point, Jenna had no idea he was scamming her.]

Jenna: I am sorry to ask you this, but do you have an accent? [Jenna asked this because he was supposed to be a US soldier, but she detected an accent in his writing.] The first man I fell in love with when I was in my twenties told me he was divorced for eight years. He had a sister, Diane, who was pregnant. I used to send food up to her all the time. I dated him for nine months, and at the end of the nine months, I found out that his sister Diane was actually his wife, Linda, who was having his baby.

The truth goes a long way with me. I gave him a chance to tell me what went on, and he never did. When I found out that he lied to me, after cussing him out, I never talked to him again. He did reach out to me through the years and asked me for forgiveness. I couldn't do it then, but in an off chance that he comes across this book and reads it, I do forgive him because I choose not to carry hate in my body. But I will never forget how he made me feel.

Eric: I understand. Okay, babe. What time is it over there? [Nice way to deflect the conversation.] And what are you doing at the moment? It is late here. I'm about to rest for a short while. I will text you before going out on patrol. I love you so much, honey. Kisses and hugs to you, my sweet baby. [At this point, he knew that if Jenna found out, she just wouldn't talk to him again. And this was fine with him because he would just find another woman to terrorize.]

Jenna: Sweet dreams to you. It is 6:30 p.m. here.

Jenna sent him a picture of her car, which you could hardly see because of all the snow on it. She had to dig herself out.

Eric: LOL. No, drive it like that, baby. It will be fun. LOL. You are the most beautiful woman in the world. I am so happy you are in my life and glad to say you are mine. Good morning, my sweetheart with a long kiss with the first moment of the day. I wish you a good morning. You are my darling wife. I love you so much, baby. I can't wait to live with you. [He meant to say that he couldn't wait to live without Jenna sending him money.]

Jenna: Good morning. XOXO.

Eric: Good morning, baby. How was your night?

Jenna: It was okay. It has been a very busy day, and I had to shovel my car out this morning. So I got up extra early to do it. I am preparing for a meeting tonight. My body aches from shoveling. Thank you for the song that you sent to me. It was beautiful.

Eric: You are always welcome, baby.

Jenna: Where did you come from?

Eric: I will be here, waiting for your message. I miss you so much. My body and heart just can't stop reaching out for you. Thank you so much for giving me the opportunity to love you. I promise to love and spend the rest of my life with you. I wanna wake up every morning and see you lying beside me in bed. I never thought I would find a woman to love again ever since I lost my wife. I thank God every second of my life for bringing you into my life. [Jenna was probably sending money to his wife.] I love you so much, baby.

Jenna: I love you too. [Hook, line, and sinker.]

Eric: What are you doing at the moment? I can see you are busy. Text me when you are less busy.

Jenna: Sorry, I am straight out with the catch-up work and the meeting tonight.

Eric: It is okay, honey. Text me when you are less busy. I love you so, so, so, so much.

Jenna: Can you take a selfie and send it to me? I want to see you. [At this point, Jenna was a little concerned. She thought, *Maybe he is scamming me.*]

Eric: Baby, I thought I told you we are not allowed to using cell phones or even make video calls for security reasons. Text me when you are less busy, okay, baby?

March 14, 2018

Eric: I really miss you, baby. I wanna rest a short while. Text me when you are free. I love you so much. I love you too much.

Jenna: Hi, Eric. I just got home from the APC meeting. We learned about TAVRs and WATCHMANs, and the guy that gave the speech was fantastic. It was a great meeting.

Eric: I am sorry for the stress, babe. Good morning to you. Babe, am sorry you had a stressful day at work yesterday. Honey, I miss you so much. I hope you slept well.

Then Eric sent Jenna a good-morning picture.

Eric: Your love brightens up my day because you always rock my world. I love the way you cherish and love me. I love you beyond the stars. Good morning, honey. I am keeping you forever. Honey, I love you. Honey. Hello? Honey, where are you? I haven't heard from you the whole day. That makes me worried.

Jenna: Sorry. I have been in and out of audits all day today. I have a huge headache and am working on another audit and getting charges in.

Eric: Baby, you read my message, but you did not reply. Why didn't you?

Jenna: I was in the car, driving. I just got home now.

Eric: How was work today?

Jenna: Crazy busy. How about you?

Eric: I wish I was there to prepare dinner for you. I would be the happiest man on earth.

Jenna: You sound too good to be true. Are you really the man you sent me a picture of? [At this point, Jenna was stressed out over a job that had a huge amount of stress and this man who she was sending money to and did not know.]

Eric: Baby, why are you thinking like that? I can't pretend to be who I am not, okay? Is it because am expressing how I feel to you?

Eric sent two pictures of this very handsome man with chiseled cheekbones.

Jenna: No, I don't want you to lie to me, okay? So you are the real deal?

Eric: These are my most recent photos. They are selfies I took by myself. Believe me, I'm not going to risk myself for this again because taking those pictures could cost me my life and my job. If I am caught, I am going to have the UN to contend with. I didn't use my phone, though, because we agreed that we would not be allowed to use our phones, so I asked an Afghanistan friend of mine to help me with this. And I am never going to do that again.

Jenna: Okay, sorry. I have been hurt before. I had a guy that stalked me and would not leave me alone. He kept trying to get onto my Facebook, and when you wouldn't send me your picture, I thought it was him. [Jenna's intuition was off, but she knew there was something not aligned.]

Eric: Baby, I am not him—not going to lie to you in any way, okay? Honey, sorry if the pictures are not that clear. It is night here, honey. I just want to be happy with you. I don't need any heartbreaks okay, honey?

Jenna: You got in touch with me through Facebook, then all of a sudden, FB was gone. I get what you are doing is classified, but the first guy that lied to me said he was part of the FBI and couldn't tell me anything. He was lying to me the whole time. So forgive me. I don't want to be hurt or taken advantage of.

Eric: Baby, I am sorry about that, okay? I swear on my honor. I don't have another woman. My wife died a long time ago, and I just have my one son. And that is all. I am never gonna hurt you, okay, honey?

Jenna: Okay. Your picture is very handsome. How tall are you?

Eric: Thank you, babe. I am 5'11" tall, and you? I don't know about my weight anymore because I lost some because of stress.

Jenna: I am 5'3" and 5'5" with heels on.

Eric: Wow, cool, that is nice. I thought you were taller than me and that I would have to stand on a chair to kiss you. LOL.

Jenna: I don't know about my weight because my scale is broken.

Eric: LOL.

Jenna: I am trying to lose some. I need to lose my belly fat.

Eric: Good but not too much, baby.

Jenna: I want to lose it in my belly, thighs, and ass.

Eric: Wow, cool, baby.

Jenna: I had an audit in work last week. They only looked at ten visits I told them two years ago I needed help with in-patient leveling, and I needed some guidance with these codes. So what did they do? They audited me on it. Instead of helping me, they do an audit on something they know I am going to fail at. Grrr. I am starting to send my resume out now. This is getting ridiculous!

Eric: Baby, remember what I told you about Jerry [his son]. It really gets me worried always, honey.

Jenna: I don't know how much I will have to give you. I get paid next Thursday.

Eric: It is okay, baby.

Jenna: Don't you get paid there?

Eric: No, baby, I only get paid when my mission is over. [This is not the truth. Army men do get paid regardless. Jenna has been told since, but do not let them tell you this. Look into it if you don't believe me.]

Jenna: I knew a guy that was in the Army, and he always had money. Has it changed?

Eric: Baby, not on a mission like this, okay? We are only paid when our mission is over.

Jenna: Gotcha. Sorry, hon, I wish I knew how to get some money to him.

Eric: What do you mean?

Jenna: I wish I had a paycheck to help Jerry out. You need to get some sleep. You have been up all night. I feel bad that I am keeping you up.

Eric: It is okay. You helped him out on his birthday, and I know you don't have it with you at the moment, honey, okay? I will text you in the morning before going out on patrol, okay, honey?

Jenna: I have to pay a car payment and taxes of over $800. If I am going to help you and Jerry out, I have to work overtime.

Eric: Okay, baby. Good night and sweet dreams.

Jenna: Sweet dreams to you too. I am sorry I judged you. You are not like anyone I have known. You are magnificent.

Jenna sent a black-and-white photo of her in her twenties from when she was in the John Robert Powers modeling school.

Eric: Baby, you know my life was colorless, but you fill my life with beautiful colors of happiness. Good morning, my beautiful woman, my heartbeat. After meeting you, I became worthy and a better person in this world. Thank you for coming into my life. I wish you a very wonderful day. Baby, please call on me if you are stressed out. Kisses and hugs, baby.

Jenna: Hi, I just woke up to take the dog out. It is still night here for a little bit, so I am going back to sleep.

Jenna: Good morning again. I am at work now.

Eric: Hello, baby. I am back from patrol, honey. I miss you so very much. How is work today?

Eric sent Jenna some songs.

Jenna: thank you for the song. It helped. It is extremely stressful here, but I can handle it. And I am learning so much. I am thinking of you.

Jenna sent Eric a song.

Eric: Wow, I love the songs, honey. Thank you so much. There may be many beautiful girls but none as beautiful as you. The day you entered my life, my whole world was filled with happiness. You always stood by my side, and I promise that I will shower you with all my love and time. Good morning to you. Every day I wake up and choose to be happy because you give me a reason to. I love you so much and am stuck on you forever. I wish you a wonderful day.

Jenna: Awww, you are so wonderful. I definitely dreamed you up. [Jenna believed God found the man for her then.] I asked for a handsome husband. I couldn't have asked for anyone as perfect as you. I love you. And I asked for a passionate person.

March 17, 2018

Jenna: Happy St. Patrick's Day. I hope you are having some fun with your friends or your troops.

March 18, 2018

Eric: Thank you so much. The signal here is so bad, honey. Every morning is a new beginning. Always make your day a great one because it is God's gift and blessing.

Jenna: I am not sure if it is night or morning there. It is 4:50 a.m. here. Just thinking of you and hoping you are safe.

Eric: Hello, baby. I am here now. I am sorry. We went on an emergency meeting, honey.

Jenna: Not a problem. It must be late.

Eric: Yes, it is late, but I am not happy right now. 😣 😣 😣 [When you see crying emojis, take it from me and run like hell.]

Eric: Baby, do you remember when I told you about my money that I deposited in the security company Ghana West Africa? [Jenna did check the site, and the site was a legitimate site.]

Jenna: Yes, I do remember. That is where I sent the money to Whitney, correct?

Eric: Yes, honey, but there is a problem right now. I received an email from the security company an hour ago. They said I should come for my money. They said the company is having problems with the board of trustees, so they will be folding up any moment from now, my love. Babe, are you with me?

Jenna: OMG, that is horrible.

Eric: Yes, honey, I am about to lose everything that I have labored for. Baby, you know I am still in the war zone. And there is no way they are going to deliver it to me here in the war zone, honey. So I really need your help on this, love.

Jenna: How can I help you?

Eric: Baby, I need you to help me contact the security company and ask them what is required for them to deliver my box. Honey, this is money I planned to use in starting up a very big business when I get retired, and I can't afford to lose such a huge amount of money. Honey, we are talking about 2,200,000.

Eric: Baby, are you with me?

Jenna: Yes, driving. What is the number?

Eric: Honey, I am going to send you the company link right now so you can get in touch with the company. Okay, baby?

Eric: Http://courier.crudexpress.com. [Eric then wrote what he wanted Jenna to say after clicking the link.]

Eric: "This is Jenna. I am contacting you on behalf of my fiancé. Gen Eric has requested that I contact you for the consignment box he deposited in your security company. I need to know what is required for it to be delivered to me in my home country. Also indicated that the delivery documents of the consignment's box will be able to provide them to me.

Thank you,

Eric Q"

Eric: Baby, this is the company link and how you are going to address the company, okay, honey? Text me when you get home so I will tell you what to do, okay?

Jenna: Okay. I'm at the doctor's office, coding.

Eric: Okay, honey. Text me when you get home, okay, honey?

Jenna: Okay. That is a lot of money. I can open up a bank account for you for your money to be deposited into. I would just need to have your information to be able to do that.

Eric: Honey, no, the company won't do that okay? [That was because the company was him, who wanted money.] The company agents are going to deliver my box to you, okay?

Eric: They will want to take some information from you to ensure my box was delivered to you safely, okay, honey? There are some documents you will have to sign before the company hands over my box to you, okay, honey?

Eric: Baby, do you understand me?

Jenna: What about Whitney? She is in Ghana right now. Can't she pick this box up for you? Why do they want to get rid of the money in their bank? It makes no sense.

Eric: Can't you understand? It is not a bank. It is a security company, and they will be folding up at any moment now. Jerry's teacher can't get there because they are living in another West Africa company. Okay, do you understand me now?

Jenna: Yes, I sent the text you wrote. I copied and pasted it and sent it to the link you wanted me to send it to. Now what do I do?

Eric: Baby, you have to contact the company. I hope you include your Gmail so the company can get back to you.

Jenna: I think I did.

Eric: Okay, baby. They are gonna get back to you soon, okay, honey? But you are going to find little amount of money for the delivery fee, okay, honey? And don't worry about that, okay? I am going to pay you double when I am out of here. All I want right now is for my box to be safe with you, okay?

Eric: Honey, when you sent the money, what did they say to you?

Jenna: I just sent it an hour ago. I haven't seen anything in my Gmail yet.

Eric: Honey, I don't know for now, but they are going to get back to you soon. I believe it won't be much to get the box out.

Jenna: Okay, what do I do with it after? Do you want the funds in a credit union?

Eric: Honey, just keep it safe for me. I planned on using it for a private house investment.

Jenna: How do I keep that much money safe?

Eric: Honey, you can deposit it in the bank when the company delivers it to you.

Jenna: I will need your information.

Eric: Oh yes, I will do that when it is delivered to you. Did you contact the company?

Jenna: I cut, copied, and pasted your text and my name into the system.

Eric: Okay. How was your day?

Jenna: Stressful.

Eric: LOL. I am sorry about that.

Jenna: I came home. I had so much anxiety from what you are going through and what I am about to do for you that I can't think. So I came home and am upstairs by myself. How did you make all that money?

Eric: Wow, I am sorry for disturbing you with my issue. I am in my resting room, thinking about you, honey.

Jenna: You are not disturbing me. I just don't know what to expect.

Eric: Honey, it is a crude-oil-and-gold business I got involved in some time ago. I went on a peace mission in West Africa.

Jenna: I was more upset about you losing your fortune if I didn't step up and help you. [Someone with $2,200,000 does not need someone helping them with money.]

Eric: Okay, honey. Have you eaten and taken your meds?

Jenna: I don't take meds. You must be thinking of someone else? 😆 😆 😆 I never even smoked a joint. I drink wine. That is it.

Eric: Oh no, honey, I do take meds every day so I will be healthy for another day, so I thought you do the same.

Jenna: Do you mean vitamins?

Eric: Oh yes, honey, and pharmaceuticals for headaches and body pains.

Jenna: Please don't worry about your investments. I will bring them right to the bank for you. [As you can see, there wasn't anybody with money. It was all Jenna's money.]

Eric: I know you will, honey. That has really given me sleepless nights, so what is next?

Jenna: I can't believe I am doing this. I have only known you for a week, and already I have sent your son a present and accepted to help you with your money situation. This is not something I would do for a person that I haven't met yet. But I feel you are a good, trusting person. I don't feel like you are one of those scam artists that everyone hears about. I pray I can help you with what you need. I hope to meet you one day.

Jenna: I am going to study and have a glass of wine. Go to sleep. I will be audited again in the morning.

Eric: Oh, thank you so much, honey. God bless you. I can't wait to meet you in person as well.

Jenna: I looked up Eric Q, and I didn't see any Caucasian men, only African American men and one serial killer. YIKES. He had your last name but not your first.

Eric: LOL. My profile is hidden for now, honey, because I am still in the war zone. Good night and sweet dreams.

Jenna: Okay, I believe you.

Eric: I love you so much, honey.

Jenna: Thank you for the beautiful red-rose picture. Thank you, Eric, and thank you, St. Theresa. Thank you for the lovely song as well. Good night, sweetheart.

Jenna: Good morning to you. It is night here for me.

Eric: In the morning, the sunlight makes you shine some more. In the morning, you have an amazing grace on your face. It gives me a reason to smile. I am wishing you a good morning, love. I have told this message to the sweetest person in the world, and now you are reading it. Good morning, my love. How was your night? I hope you slept well, my love. I love you so much, honey. I wish you a very wonderful day today.

Jenna: I wish you a wonderful day as well.

Eric: I am back from patrol now, honey. So how is your day? I miss you so much.

Jenna: It's okay. I am tired. I didn't sleep well.

Eric: Oh, I am so sorry about that, okay, my love? What is the time over there? What are you doing at the moment?

Jenna: I'm working. It's 10:11 a.m.

Eric: Have you heard from the security company yet?

Jenna: Not yet.

Eric: Okay, keep checking your email. If I were given the chance to make one wish, I'd only wish for one thing. I would wish that we would grow old together and that our love would last forever.

Eric: Text me when you are free.

Jenna: I am home. What a crazy day, ugh!

Eric: So sorry you had a rough day, baby. Take your bath, eat, and then text me.

Jenna: I didn't see anything from the security company, and all I got for phone calls was for my car payment and scam-likely calls.

Eric: But I sent an email to them, and they said they replied to you.

Jenna: I am looking at all my emails now, and I don't see it.

Eric: Look at the email that you used to contact the company.

Jenna: That is what I am doing now. Do you know what the company's name is? I may be able to search it.

Eric: I don't understand. Search it where, honey? It's Crude Express Security Company, okay, honey?

Jenna: Oh, my Gmail account. I just looked at it and the messages, and someone was trying to access my account. The other message was someone wanting me to sign up for a webinar, nothing to do with a security thing.

Eric: Baby, I have contacted the company a few hours ago. They said they have replied you, and they said the delivery fee costs $1,200. Honey, I am so confused right now. And I don't know what else to do, baby.

Jenna: I don't have that kind of money. I am sorry I don't see it in my Gmail. I searched it. That would probably be my whole check.

Eric: Baby, I understand. But do you want me to lose such an amount of money, honey? You will get back the money you spend in receiving it when it is delivered to you, okay, honey? This is my life savings we are talking about. Please, please do all you can to help me out.

Jenna: I don't want you to lose anything, but I am telling you my check won't be that much with my health insurance coming out. I get paid in only two-week increments. I understand what you are saying, but I cannot come up with that kind of money in one week. To me that is not a small amount. I have bills to pay. I am sorry.

Eric: Baby, please, I will pay you back double. I will also give you 10 percent if you give me the money. And you really don't know how I feel at the moment, baby. I am about to lose $2,00,000. Honey, please.

Jenna: I don't want your money. That is yours. I don't know what my check will be. I will have to see.

Eric: Okay, honey. Please do all you can to help me out and help get my box out.

Jenna: I wish I could make money appear out of thin air. If you have all of this money, why can't you pay the fees with your money? Why can't you pay with your check? Then when it comes here, I can put all of it in a bank for you.

Eric: I know you don't want my money, but it is my money. And I will do anything I want with it. And I am gonna give you 10 percent of it. Please don't say no, my love.

Eric: Baby, I can't do that from here. There are some documents I need to sign, and that's why I am seeking for your help. Things are getting worse here in Afghanistan, and the company agent said they can't risk their life like that. Baby, are you sleeping already?

Jenna: No, I am not sleeping.

Eric: Kisses and hugs to you.

Jenna: You too, and thank you for the song you sent. It was nice.

Eric: My love, when you are not with me, I don't feel good. With you I feel so complete. My beautiful wife, I love you so very much. I wish you an amazing morning, and have a wonderful day today.

As long as Jenna was paying and getting him the money he needed, she was his beautiful wife, his queen, and his baby. As soon as the money was not available to him, she was not any of these endearing qualities to him.

Eric: My dear love, I can't imagine my life without your because I love you so much. How was your night? I hope you slept well.

Jenna: I am about to drive to work. How late is it there?

Eric: Okay, honey. It is 3:13 p.m.

Jenna: It is 7:32 a.m. here.

Eric: Text me when you are free, baby.

Jenna: Crazy, stressful, busy day. Now I am watching a CD.

Eric: Sorry about that, okay? Where are you? Are you home now?

Jenna: No, watching a CD.

Eric: Sorry about that, okay? Text me when you are home. I love you very much. Hugs and kisses.

Jenna: Hi, I had to take a test again.

Eric: It's okay, honey. I know you are very busy. My main dream is to wake up next to you. Soon it will come true. Good morning, my love. I just wanted to tell you that I am the person that thinks about you in the morning and before going to bed. Good morning to you, baby.

Jenna: Good morning to you. I love the song you sent me. I have never heard it before. "When you are feeling you can't go on, you never live alone no and you live in me."

Eric: I am glad you do, my love. Are you not going to work today?

Jenna: I am at work today. I came in early. I have an interview at 3:30 p.m.

Eric: Okay, text me when you are free.

Jenna: Okay. I'm crazy busy.

Eric: How is your day going? I miss you so much.

Jenna: How is your day going? Is it nighttime there?

Eric: I am not doing good, honey. I miss you so very much.

Jenna: What is going on?

Eric: Honey, I received an email from the security company, and they said there are only a few days remaining. I'm so confused right now.

Jenna: Why the confusion?

Eric: Honey, I don't wanna lose my box. Baby, are you there with me? Baby, are you still at work?

Jenna: I just got home. I had an interview today. We shall see.

Eric: Wow, cool. How was the interview?

Jenna: I know I can't afford $1,200. I wish I could help you. I have a car payment, my son is moving out, I am helping him, and I have credit cards I have to pay for. I have been behind in trying to help my son, and I don't expect money back from him.

Eric: Baby, I understand. But if my box is delivered to you, you can give our son money from it. Then you can always make other payments from it, baby.

Jenna: I respect the soldiers so much and all they do for us. If I had it, I would give it. I have a little saved up to get out of the place. I am in, but if I give you that, then that is all I have.

Eric: Please, honey. Honey, I will pay you back in double please, baby. Please. 😢 😢 😢 [It's always the crying emojis.]

Jenna: I will put your box in the bank. Maybe the person who delivers it could go to the bank with me.

Eric: Baby, the company agent won't agree to that because most of their customers have run away with their money through that process.

Jenna: He can come with me in my car, and I will drive him back in his car.

Eric: Honey, the company agent won't move until the payment is made. I have sent an email to them, and they said no to that, honey. That is why I am so confused.

Jenna: Why are you confused? Because he said no?

Eric: Yes, honey.

Jenna: I don't know what to tell you, but $1,200 is all I have in my account. It is the only nest egg I have. I would have to close out my account.

* * * * *

The mere fact that Eric was asking for the exact amount that I have in my Acorns account was a little unsettling. It is also the same amount my sister asked for months later. What is it with $1,200? My sister believed that I stole boots and clothes from her years before. I remember my mother giving me gloves that she had while she was living in Arizona, but I never ever remember taking her clothes and boots from her. The fact that I had told her that I would give her $1,200. I did sleep in her room while she was away in Arizona years ago. She had boxes all over the place, and I never touched any of the boxes. I only slept in her room. Years later, my son went down and stayed with my mother and father, and they moved all of the boxes up in the attic and downstairs in the basement. Now I was thinking that it may be my sister scamming me.

* * * * *

Eric: Baby, please, you will get your money back as soon as you receive my box. Please, honey. Baby, are you with me?

Jenna: Yes, I am with you. What is in this box? It doesn't have anything illegal in it, does it? LOL.

Eric: Baby, it's a briefcase containing $2,000,000, okay? And no, there are no other things in it, just a few documents you are going to sign, okay, honey?

Jenna: What bank do I go to? Do you want it to go into a credit union?

Eric: Baby, all I want is for it to be safe with you. You can put it in any bank you want, okay, baby?

Jenna: Okay.

Eric: I just want it to be out of West Africa, okay?

March 24, 2018

Eric: Honey, when will you be paid? So you will send an email to the company, okay, baby?

Jenna: What time is it there? You need your sleep.

Eric: The time here is 4:11 a.m. I haven't slept.

Jenna: Sorry, I didn't know it was so late.

Eric: Baby, you don't need to be, okay? I was so worried. That is why I couldn't sleep.

Jenna: What is your address? So when I go to the bank, I can give them the information.

Eric: Baby, I am here now. I am sorry I went on an emergency call. Okay, honey. Baby, are you still with me?

* * * * *

Emergency call? Now I am thinking it is my ex-husband who is behind this because he was an EMT. Talk about being paranoid. I never did find out who was behind this scamming, and I will never ever know.

* * * * *

Jenna: I am up but I am tired. You must be exhausted.

Eric: I will try to get some sleep now, okay, honey? I will text you in the morning. Good night and sweet dreams, baby.

Jenna: Okay, I am going to sleep too. Sweet dreams.

Eric: I woke up thousands of miles away from you, but it doesn't matter because you are in my heart. My main dream is to wake up next to you. Soon it will come true. Good morning, my love.

Eric: Good morning, gorgeous. You spoiled me with your care and kindness, and now I cannot start my day without you. Wake up. It's another day that is brought to you, baby. I love you so much.

Jenna: Good morning. XO.

Eric: Good morning, baby. How was your day today? I miss you so very much.

Jenna: Sorry, it was a busy day. I hope you are doing well.

Eric: Baby, I am still very worried. Are you home now?

Jenna: I am home. It is 10:53 p.m. I miss talking to you on here. My check is nowhere near what you need. I feel bad, and I don't know what to do.

Eric: Baby, what do you mean? Your check was nowhere near, honey? Hello? Are you there with me? What are we going to do now, my love? Is there no one you can take a loan from and pay back as soon as my box is delivered to you, baby? Please, baby, do all you can to help me out. I can't afford to lose such a huge amount of money.

Jenna: I cleared $600. I can't even make a car payment because it is more than that. I do photography on the side. I will see if anyone wants pictures done.

Eric: Baby, this is making me go crazy. Honey, this is making me lose focus in the war zone. I keep thinking, and I don't know what else to do.

Jenna: Keep your focus and don't get hurt.

Eric: Baby, you know it's a huge amount of money. It's a huge amount of money, honey. It keeps ringing in my head every minute. Text me when you are free, okay, baby?

March 23, 2018

Jenna: Okay, I will text you. I am sorry. I wish I were a rich woman, then I could give you the money. I have some money, but it won't come right away. And I have to pay in taxes. That is $1,100.

Eric: Baby, how long is that gonna be?

Jenna: I am not sure. I have never taken anything out of it before.

Eric: Baby, please do all you can, okay? I don't have much time left.

Jenna: Okay.

Eric: Baby, do you have any friend that we can borrow from and then pay back as soon as you receive the box? We will pay back with interest.

Jenna: I don't have any friend that would pay that. I have an Acorns account that has exactly $1,200. I would have to close the account. I have never taken money out of it before.

Eric: Okay, so why don't you find time to go to the bank and see what's next, honey?

Jenna: Okay. It's Friday night at 8:00 p.m. The bank is not open. I will see how to get money from my Acorns account. This is so bizarre. I have never been in the position of giving everything I have saved and the exact amount of money that I have saved to someone I have never met. I pray that this is on the up and up and that if I do this for you, I will not get in trouble for doing it. I want to believe you so bad, but if you looked at it from my perspective, you would be thinking the same thoughts. You are trusting me with your fortune, and I am honored and definitely the person you want to trust. I swear on my life I will bring it right to the bank for you. I just hope the briefcase will not be filled with newspapers. LOL.

Eric: LOL. Newspaper, hahahaha! I will never do anything to hurt your feelings, okay, baby? And I promise I am gonna surprise you, okay? I trust you with my fortune because you helped my son even when you didn't know him. I will never forget that.

Jenna: LOL. Okay.

Eric: I will forever be grateful and indebted to you.

Jenna: How is Jerry, your son, doing?

Eric: He is doing good, baby. He said he can't wait to meet you in person. Baby, what time is it over there?

Jenna: It is 8:31 p.m. What time is it where you are?

Eric: The time here is 5:01 a.m.

Eric: Oh wow, have you slept well, Eric? Tell Jerry I said hi.

Eric: Morning, my love. And no, I haven't slept yet, but I will soon because am not going out on patrol early today, honey.

Jenna: I can't wait to meet the journalist. [On Facebook, Eric told Jenna that Jerry, his son, was studying to be a journalist.]

Eric: LOL. He is a little stubborn, but I think you can handle him.

Jenna: Well, get some sleep. I am proctoring an exam tomorrow.

Eric: Oh, baby, I wish you good luck on your exam.

Jenna: If I can handle my son, I can handle anyone. I am not taking the exam. I am proctoring the exam. I need to be in the room while the people take the exam.

Eric: Oh, baby, I wish them luck. Good night and sweet dreams to you, my love.

Jenna sent two songs to Eric. The lyrics to one was "I will stand by you. I will help you through." She was not sure of the artist or the song, but she found it on YouTube. The lyrics of the other went "The place where they are."

Eric: Thank you for the song, baby. I love it. I am listening to the songs right now. Sleeping, baby.

Jenna: Good, I love the song you gave to me as well. Thank you so much.

Jenna: Is this real? I have faith that it is. Is this feeling the same as the others? No, it is not. I prayed for a man like you. I prayed for someone to get the real me and accept my flaws, dreams, and thoughts. I love that you send me songs. I pray that you like to dance, and I pray that you love the beach. I love how you send me a picture of a rose with my morning coffee. I love how I look for the perfect song to send you every day. I pray for you and your troops to be safe every day since I have met you. Thinking of you. XOXO. Good morning, love. Who would I like to be stranded with on a deserted island? That would be you, you, you.

Eric: Wow, thank you, baby. Good morning. How was your night? I hope you slept well. I miss you so much. Kisses and hugs to you, baby.

Eric sent me a song.

Jenna: That is a beautiful song. Thank you so much. I am now proctoring a five-and-a-half-hour test today.

Eric: The time is 5:15 p.m. Honey, my love, can you go to the bank today?

Jenna: I just checked the account. It will take three to six business days for the check to get to me. I can try to get a loan, but my credit has not been good since my divorce. You picked the wrong lady to romance. I'll give what I can, but I am not rich.

Eric: It's okay, honey. Let's just wait and see what happens, my love.

Jenna: I hope I don't screw this up for you. Karma is a bitch, and I don't need any bad karma.

Eric: Baby, let's just have a positive mindset about this, okay?

Jenna: Okay, yes, positive. Your pictures are so handsome. How did you find me on FB?

Eric: Wow, thank you so much, honey.

Eric: I really don't know what I was looking for then. I came across your lovely profile, and I must say God has a better purpose for us, to be with each other. I thank God for the first day I met you.

Jenna: Nala is the dog I had on my profile. We lost her on Christmas Day.

Eric: Hello, baby, how are you doing?

Jenna: Hi.

Eric: Hello, baby, how is your day going?

Jenna: Good. Watching TV. I just heard a song by Neil Diamond. I love his voice. I wanted to share it with you. This baby will be broke but will be saving your business, and that makes me happy.

Eric: Baby, I promise you won't be broke, okay? Baby, are you sure you are going to send the money to the company next week? Because the company emailed, saying that if they don't hear from me, then it's over, honey. I can't stand the chance of losing my box.

Eric: Honey, are you sleeping now?

Jenna: Yes, as soon as I get the check, I will be able to send it. Then what? I am having a glass of wine, watching TV.

Eric: I have your picture with me. I keep staring at it every night.

Eric sent Jenna back the picture of her and her dog Sydney.

Eric: You have an amazing smile, my love. I'm gonna be playing with your hair every night. I love playing with my woman's hair, and your long hair is in trouble, baby.

Jenna: Aww, you are sweet. I am flattered. I hope I don't disappoint you when we finally meet in person. I dream of that day.

Eric: Baby, I won't allow disappointment to come.

Jenna: That picture was me when I was forty-six. I am fifty-five now.

Eric: Cool, that means you are more beautiful now, baby. I keep smiling like a newborn baby each time I stare at your picture. I can't wait to meet you and treat you like the queen you are.

Jenna: I love your smile. You are so handsome. If and when we ever get together, I will have to beat women off with a stick. When I asked God for a handsome man, he came through with flying colors. When you sent that picture, I actually said *shit* out loud. LOL.

Eric: Baby, I am sorry I fell asleep. It's late, and I had a very busy day today.

Jenna: Sweet dreams, sweetheart.

Eric: Good night and sweet dreams to you, my love.

Jenna: Good night, darlin'.

Eric: I will text you before going out on patrol, when I wake up, honey.

Jenna: Get some sleep now.

Jenna: The day I met you, I didn't know how much you would touch my heart and my soul, how you would speak to me without me ever hearing your voice, how you could touch my heart without me ever having to feel you, and how could you see my soul without ever meeting me. The day I met you, you turned my world around from being dark and dismal to being full of light and hopeful.

Jenna: You have given me hope of brighter days and made me believe again. Thank you, Eric, for coming into my life. I hope you are my lifetime, but if you decide that you are not feeling the same, I am a better person for knowing you.

Eric: Honey, I thank God for bringing you into my life, and I promise to love, cherish, adore, and respect you all through my life, baby. I know am not a perfect man, but I will do all I can in this world to always make you happy because you deserve happiness all throughout the days of your life, my love. I love you so very much, and I can't wait to meet you and tell the whole world how wonderful you are to me and everyone around you.

Eric: God bless you so much for your kind heart, and I wish everyone in this world had a good and lovely heart like yours. The world has been a better place to live in, baby. I love you so much. Kisses and huge to my sweet baby.

March 25, 2018

Jenna: Wow, I keep pinching myself to see if I am awake and if this is real. I can't wait to meet you as well. XOXO.
Eric: Hello, baby. I am here now, my love. I just returned from my evening patrol, honey, and I have missed you so much.
Jenna: Yeah, it has been dreary here. I am glad you are safe.
Eric: Yes, honey. Thank you so much for your prayer, my love.
Jenna: How have you stayed single for so long?
Eric: Baby, I can't really tell about that, but I think I was so busy with my duty and haven't found another woman that makes my heart skip a beat. And now that I have, I believe this is my time to drop my past and embrace the future with you, honey. What time is it there?
Jenna: It's 10:53 a.m. right now. I am getting ready to go into work, then to the gym, and then go study.
Eric: Oh, okay, baby.
Jenna: You must have quite a past with that face and that smile. LOL.
Eric: LOL. Oh, and I believe God is smiling on me for giving me the most wonderful woman in the world. And that's you, baby.
Jenna: You must have fallen asleep.
Eric: Baby, I am here now. I was on guard duty tonight, baby.
Jenna: Hey, there you are. Yeah, I am glad you are okay.
Eric: Oh yes, I am okay.
Jenna: I went to see a friend, went to work, went to the gym, and went back to the house to study.
Eric: That's lovely, baby. I missed you the whole day.
Jenna: I missed you too.
Eric: What are your plans for tomorrow, honey?
Jenna: Working, that is it. No plans except for work. How was your meeting? Have you eaten anything?

Eric: No, not yet, baby. It's morning over here now, and I have not slept. Honey, I will take a cup of coffee before I go out on patrol.

Eric: The meeting went well, but they are trying to impose more laws here. And I really don't like it because I won't have privacy. Baby, what do you do for fun?

Jenna: I go to the gym and run outside, on the beach.

Eric: I will be joining you. Soon I will be out of here, honey.

Jenna: Yeah? Is your term up soon?

Eric: Yes, I think so, but I have not heard any news about it yet. But I believe that soon I will be out of here, honey.

Jenna: Yeah! You are coming back to the States.

Eric: Yes, baby, and then I will be returning from my duty so I can live a normal life like everyone else and so I can give you all the attention you need, honey. I didn't give my wife the attention she needed, and it hurts me so much when I think about it. And I am not making that same mistake again, honey.

Jenna: I am sure your wife loved you very much, and I am sure that you gave her as much attention as you could have. I know she cherished the moments with you. When you love someone, it doesn't matter the amount of time you have. What matters is the quality of time you give. Don't beat yourself up about it. You did the best you could for your family, and she knows that.

Eric: Oh, thank you so much for your lovely words, honey. They made me smile.

Jenna: This makes me think of my ex-husband and how he didn't do a lot, just worked, fished, and hunted. He didn't ever want to be around the family. Even when my friends and family were here, he would always just leave the room without a hello or anything.

Jenna: It made me independent, I had to do a lot of things around the house myself and when I walked away from him because of how he treated all of us I was done.

Jenna: I hear that it made him a much nicer person. He is remarried and from only one incident with his new wife reaching out to me, she let me know that her husband was not "paying my son a dime," as she put it. I texted her back to let her know that our firstborn was our son and that what her husband and our son decided between them had nothing to do with me. She was a little erratic, so I ended up having to let my ex know that his new wife would, as she told me, throw him out of the house if he gave our son one dime. He told me not to worry, and he did end up helping him out. I wouldn't have wanted to be in his home that night.

Jenna: The whole time throughout our marriage, I would pray that he would get his karma one day. I think I prayed a little too much. I did apologize years later for praying that because I think he has someone ten times worse than he was.

Eric: Wow, that is going to be a lesson for him. I will bet he will change for good. I have a very hard and headachey day ahead of me, honey.

Jenna: From what? I hear he has changed for the better. I haven't seen him in years. We all have our paths to choose.

Eric: Oh yes, I believe in God's plan, baby. I have to rest for a short while before going on patrol.

Jenna: Okay, you rest. Know that I am thinking of you.

Eric: Thank you, baby. And thinking of you keeps me going here, my love. Rest well, my honey.

Jenna: You too, babe.

Eric: The early morning is the best moment of the day. It's when I show my love for you, baby. Good morning, my cute, cute woman. Have a nice day. I think about you always. You are my true love who gives me many things in life. You are always with me, and I am always with you.

Jenna: I just got up. XOXO. My wish for you this Monday morning, or evening, in your case, is that no harm will come to you.

Eric: Hello, baby. I am back from patrol now. My love, how is your day?

Jenna: My day is extremely stressful.

Eric: LOL. I understand, baby. Don't stress yourself much, okay?

Jenna: On the good side, I have another face-to-face interview coming up. Get some sleep now, sweetheart. XOXO.

Eric: Hello, baby. How are you doing today? I received an email. They can't wait too much longer.
Jenna: The money is not out of the bank yet.

March 27, 2018

Jenna: I must admit something to you. When you asked for ₵750 and I didn't have it, I agonized about it because I didn't have it for Jerry. Then right after you needed ₵750, at that point, I am sorry to say this, I thought you were trying to con me? I hope you will forgive my thoughts, but my thinking is that you are a soldier fighting in a war for us. And I would rather give you money and help you out than agonize over losing a fortune because of me. If I give you the money and you stay, I will know you are the real deal. But if you chose to leave, then I have helped someone I care about, and that to me is priceless.
Eric: Okay, I see. It's okay. I am not angry about it. You know we are all humans, and we have different ways of thinking.
Jenna: Karma comes back to those who are good. My karma has not shown up yet, but I believe it will soon.
Jenna: My son was going to join the army, but he decided not to. In a way, I wish he had gone, but when you tell me of the soldiers losing their lives, it makes me sad. God forgive me, but I am glad he didn't go. I worry about you there. I hope someday we can meet face-to-face.
Eric: I have never been in any other relationship ever since I lost my wife. It's not that I don't want a relationship, but it is hard to find a sincere woman that will love you for who you are and not what you are. We have only been together for a short period, and yet I feel safe with you. All my life, I have prayed for a woman who will love me the way I love her, a woman who will look me straight in the eye and tell me if I am right or wrong. I love you so, so much, Jenna Nothing is ever going to change that. I keep praying to God, asking him to guide and protect me until I am out of here so we can meet. I pray God continues to see us through.

Jenna: That made me smile. I love you too even though we haven't met. I love you. Looking at the picture of your face is awesome. I couldn't have dreamt you up any better. I believe you are my good karma coming to me. I have prayed and prayed for a man like you for a long time. There are very few of you on this earth.

Eric: Baby, you made me realize there is still so much for me to live for. Most of the soldiers here have lost hope because they keep thinking they might die out there, but talking to you [texting Jenna] makes me different from them. It makes me believe I have a lot of responsibilities to take care of when I am out of here. God will keep guiding me, honey.

Jenna: Oh yes, God will guide you. Instead of thinking bad, try to think of good. Keep a vision in your mind of you being out and the troops coming home.

Eric: Oh yes, that is what I keep praying for, honey. Baby, let me know when the company has replied to you. Baby, have you heard any news about your check?

Jenna didn't see Eric's text because she was sending pictures of the *Law of Attraction* book to Eric.

Jenna: Hopefully, you can see the pages. I have been reading this so much that the pages are falling apart.

Eric: Oh yes, I see it clearly now. I will be going through it.

Jenna: I will send you more. They are very inspirational.

Eric: Thank you, honey, for the inspirational quotes. Baby, are you sure you are going to get the check this week? I feel very unstable about my box.

Jenna: Say this every day. I wrote it for you.

Jenna: "I, Eric, will live to my fullest potential. I cherish every day. I make new friends that I hold dear to my heart. I am living with loving, caring people that want the best for me. I have a beautiful life, and everyone around me has peace and tranquility. No one dies, and everyone I care about lives. Next month, the war will be over, and I will get to go home to my family. My box is safe, and I will get my money."

Eric: Wow, touching, my love. Thank you for that, honey. I love you so much, baby.

Jenna: Yes, hon, I got an email saying that funds were removed from the account.

Eric: Okay, babe. I don't feel tired when I talk to you, baby, but I have to rest for a short while because I have a very busy day ahead of me. I will text you before going out on patrol.

Jenna: Okay, sweetheart. I am trying to send you an album.

Eric: Okay, baby. Good night. Sweet dreams. Kisses and hugs to you.

Jenna: While you were sleeping, I was thinking of you and praying that you would have a beautiful night's sleep.

Eric: Oh, thank you so much, love. I thought about you the whole day. You are the first thought of my day. I never want to forget you, my love. You are my addiction. I can't live without you anymore. I want to wake up in your arms. Good morning, my love. My love, I miss you so much. I dream every night about you, baby. I want to see you early in the morning. Do you know love is the meeting of two souls?

Jenna: Good morning. Thank you for the beautiful coffee picture and the flowers. You must be on patrol.

Eric: I feel so worried about it, honey.

Jenna: Can I get in touch with them?

Eric: Oh yes, honey. Send an email about the delay. That will be better, baby. You still have the company's details?

Jenna: What is the email address?

Eric: You can't send an email. You have to go through a link.

Jenna: Okay, what is the link?

Eric: Honey, you don't have it with you anymore?

Jenna: I have to look it up?

Eric: Oh yes, I still have it here with me, honey, and am going to send it right away. Http.//courier.crudexpress.com. Baby, that is the company's link again.

Jenna: Okay.

Eric: Baby, let me know when you are done with it.

Jenna: Done.

Eric: Oh, okay. They will get back to you once they receive your emails. What time is it over there?

Jenna: It's 7:44 p.m.

Eric: Oh, good evening to you, baby. How was your work today?

Jenna: Very stressful.

Eric: Oh, sorry about that, baby. I wish I was there to help you out with some things.

Jenna: Awww, thank you. XOXO.

Eric: You are always welcome, honey.

Eric: Nothing yet, honey? They will reply when they receive your email, okay, honey?

Jenna: Okay. Do you feel better?

Eric: Yes, baby. Thank you so much, honey.

Jenna: Don't thank me yet. Not until they get back to us.

Eric: All right, honey.

Jenna: Just working and going to the gym. Good morning to you.

Eric: Thank you, baby. But I haven't slept yet, honey. Oh, thank you, honey. Oh no, I am sorry I am keeping you up. Please go to get some sleep. You need it, sweetheart. XOXO.

Jenna: I am sending you some Reiki and some healing Reiki music.

Eric: I love you, baby. I will text you before going out on patrol, when I wake up, honey.

Jenna: Sweet dreams. XO. Okay.

Eric: Good night. Sweet dreams. XOXO to you, my love.

Jenna: Thank you. XOXO.

Eric: I love you, baby.

Jenna: Back at you, babe. Thank you for the kisses and hugs. I hope you are sleeping, and I hope the Reiki helps. XOXO.

Eric: I love you forever. You are the only reason for living. I want to spend my full life with you always. I can't live without you. Good morning, my baby. You are the best moment of my life. Good morning, my sweetheart. How was your night? I hope you slept well.

Jenna: Good evening to you. I just woke up. XOXO. You must be sleeping or on patrol.

Eric: I'm here now, my love.

Jenna: Oh, good.

Eric: I'm sorry. I had a very busy and stressful day, my love. I miss you so much, honey.

Jenna: You do? That is nice to hear.

Eric: How are you doing today? What time is it?

Jenna: It is 1:25, and I am okay.

Eric: Text me when you are free, okay, baby?

Jenna: Okay, I will text you when I am out.

Eric: I am missing you so much.

Jenna: I just got home and changed. I got a call yesterday about a second interview, so there is light at the end of the tunnel. How was your day today?

Eric: Oh, everything went well, honey.

Jenna: That is good.

Eric: All right. Take a bath and eat, and then text me when you are done.

Jenna: I am not taking a bath. I am going to study. You must be thinking of someone else. LOL.

Eric: I am not chatting with anyone else, honey. I will never do that, baby.

Jenna: You can chat. I am not jealous unless you give me something to be jealous about. LOL.

Eric: Baby, I don't want to chat with anyone else. You are the only woman that holds the key to my joy and happiness, honey. I love, cherish, adore, and respect you, baby. Are you still going out?

Jenna: If you ever see me jealous of someone, then you will know you have me hook, line, and sinker. I am the kind of girl that if I am dating you, then you get all my attention. I don't like to play games. If I am out with you, I am out with you and you alone.

Eric: That is so lovely, baby.

Jenna: I do love to meet people. Like if you are on a date and sitting in a bar and a couple sits beside you, I am the kind of person to start a conversation with them.

Eric: Baby, I don't have friends. I once did. Then they all turned their backs on me when I needed them most. Now I only have soldier boys like me. I take them as my friends, but you are my woman. And I will forever hold you high in my heart, baby. I can't wait for the day I come to meet you, honey.

Jenna: Well, I hope you have friends when you are with me. Just because someone goes out of your life doesn't mean that all of them will. I have had friends I have walked away from, and I have friends that I haven't spoken to in years. But as soon as we see one another, it is like we never left. You just need to meet the right friends.

Eric: Why did they turn their backs on you?

Jenna: I have a poem that I think will help you put friendship into a different perspective.

Eric: Okay, honey, bring it on.

Jenna sent Eric the poem "A Reason, a Season, or a Lifetime."

Eric: Wow, that is lovely, baby. I will have second thoughts about friends. Thank you. Honey, tell me about your work. Today mine was rougher and more stressful than before, and sometimes I just wish there is something I can do to end this war.

March 28, 2018

I want to say that my burning desire right now is to bring these people to justice and get this book into as many hands as I can to help stop this from happening to innocent people. Eric played with my emotions and extracted all the money he could from me.

* * * * *

Jenna: While you were sleeping, I was thinking of you and praying that you would have a beautiful night's sleep. XOXO.

Eric: Okay, thank you so much, my love. I think about you the whole day. You are the first thought of my day. I never want to forget you, my love. Good morning, my love. You are my addiction. I can't live without you anymore. I want to wake up in your arms. Good morning, my love. How was your night? I hope you slept well.

Jenna: TTYL. I am at work. I hope you are okay.

Eric: Hello, baby. I am back from patrol. I miss you so much. Text me when you are free. Kisses and hugs to you, my love.

Jenna: Thank you. I needed that today. It's a rough one. Sorry, I am still working. How was your day today? Did you sleep?

Eric: No, I haven't slept. I am still waiting to wish you a good night. Honey, have you heard any news about the check?

Jenna: I know they took the money out, but I'm not sure if it is in my mailbox. I am not home. What do I do when it comes?

Eric: Honey, keep it in the bank or anywhere it will be safe.

Jenna: I am home, and the check is not in the mail yet. But it will be coming.

Eric: Baby, can't you call them so they will give you the exact date? Welcome, home, baby. How was your day today? Baby, are you with me?

Jenna: Yes, I am here. It is not in the bank. I looked into an investment that every time I wrote a check, they round up the change. It is not in my bank. I was investing for my future so I can get out of this house, and I was halfway there when you waltzed into my life. Now I am trusting you with pretty much every penny that I saved to help you. I will take a look.

Eric: Baby, I was thinking, what if we buy a house so we can live comfortably baby? Or will you move in with me to my house?

Jenna: Yeah, it's on its way, the check.

Eric: I have a big house in Florida, baby.

Eric: Oh, that's nice, honey. Will it get here by tomorrow?

Jenna: I love Florida, and my son loves Florida. I would move in a heartbeat. I hate the cold and the snow. I am hoping it will be there tomorrow. It should be. It was on its way on Monday.

Eric: Oh, that is nice, baby. We are going to live in Florida together, my love, and we are all going to be happy together, baby. I have a pool in my compound, honey.

Eric: Baby, did the company give you an address that you are going to send the money to?

Jenna: No, they are sending the check to me, so it should be here soon. I am thinking tomorrow. I will have to open an account. Something pulled from my account, and I have a negative balance now, UGH. If I put the money in there, I will be short $150. This snow is killing me. Every time I have worked overtime, I haven't use it for a snow day.

Jenna: You haven't even met me yet. How do you know this? LOL. You are so good.

Jenna: Maybe you won't like by Bostonian accent or my body. LOL. I love that you are thinking that way, but you are with a bunch of men right now. Once you get back to the States, you will have your pick of women. I will be standing at the end of the line.

Jenna was overweight at this point and at a low vibration from everything that happened in her life. Jenna is now forty pounds thinner (and it is 2019 as I am writing this). She is a whole new person, and she is in higher vibrations.

Eric: Baby, I have not met you, I know, but I believe you are nicer than your words, honey. And all I want to be is happy with you in all ways.

Jenna: That sounds so nice. I can't wait to meet you and kiss you. How do you kiss?

Eric: LOL. Baby, am a one-woman man, and I have given you all my trust, love, and attention, which I will never give to any other woman.

Eric: Baby, kissing is my favorite, and I do love a hard kiss, honey.

Jenna: Awww, well, I am a one-man woman when the man shows me he wants me in his life. If the man cheats or disrespects me or if he promises me things, well, then all bets are off. I believe that you and I may be soulmates.

Jenna: When I saw your picture, it was like a jolt went through me. I don't know. I just wanted to get to know you better.

Jenna: It says it's transferring to my bank, UGH! My bank has a negative balance. If I tell them to send me a check, it will take longer. This is so stressful.

Eric: Baby, I know am not perfect, and sometimes I might make mistakes. But the worst thing I can do to you, which I can't do, is cheat on you. And secondly, I can't let you walk out of my life, honey. I am indebted to you and you alone.

Eric: Honey, I meant the security company. Did they give you an address that you will use in sending the money to them so they will deliver my box to you?

Jenna was still thinking of the hard kiss that Eric liked.

Jenna: Mmmm, I love a hard kiss but not too hard. Holding the face and tongue but not a slurpy spit kiss, a grandma "peck on the lips or cheek" kiss, and not the "pucker up and turn the other cheek to the side." What is that? Ugh.

Eric: Hahahahahahahahaha!

Jenna: I didn't see anything. I pulled up the site, and this Sandy Bell from MOBE comes up. I did speak to her, and she was real. But how did that come up?

Eric: Have you not received any message from the security company yet? Have you refreshed your email?

Jenna: I am still looking for the man that when he kisses me, I will go weak in the knees.

Eric: That's me, baby.

Jenna: Mmm, you make me go weak in the knees from just looking at your picture. 😆 🩶

Jenna: I will refresh it now.

Eric: LOL. I keep smiling like a newborn baby from reading your text, honey.

Jenna: LOL. I am smiling big.

Eric: I never thought I would be this happy again when I lost my wife, but here I am feeling so blessed from having you in my life, baby.

Jenna: I feel blessed that I have you in my life as well. You know, maybe it was your wife that sent you to me. Maybe somehow she saw how lonely we were and how we tried to find love but couldn't, hmmm? What time is it, sweetheart?

Jenna: I don't see anything in my box. Once I have the money, I will call them.

Eric: I am sorry I nodded off, baby.

Eric: I have a very busy day, and the time here is 5:02 a.m. Baby, do you have the company number?

* * * * *

I wonder if his very busy day was because he was conning other women like me out of their money.

* * * * *

Jenna: Okay, sleep. We will catch up later. XO.

Eric: Thank you so much, honey. Good night and sweet dreams to you, my love. I will text you before going out on patrol, okay, honey? Baby, I will make contact with the account information, okay, honey? You just let me know when you have the money with you, okay, honey?

Jenna: Sweet dreams to you. XOXO. Okay.

Eric: I mean I will make contact with the company for the account information that you are going to send the money to, okay, baby?

Jenna: Good night, love. I am going to kiss you like I mean it, okay?

Eric: Night-night, baby. Love you too much, honey. Kisses and hugs to you, my sweet love. I love you so much, my baby. I wish you a sweet morning in this world. A kiss is a lovely trick designed by nature to close your lips. Good morning to you, honey.

Eric: I fell in love with you and will do so always. My love for you increases more when you tell me something about me. Every person has a true love in their lives. I am a lucky person of this world that has a true love. Good morning.

Eric: How was your night? I miss you so much, honey.

Jenna: You are the most wonderful man. I love you. XOXO.

Jenna: Hey, you. I have good news and bad news. Acorns transferred my money into my account. However, there was a negative balance, so I can't send $1,200. I can only send you $971.

Eric: Baby, so is the money with you now? Baby, are you there with me? I am back from patrol, my love, and I miss you so very much, honey. Text you me when you are free.

Jenna: Yeah it is in my account, but not as much as you asked for.

Eric: Honey, so they have not delivered it to you? Baby, you have to send that one to the company, and I will plead with them to proceed with the delivery, okay, honey?

Eric: Baby, are you there with me? This is so they will know we are serious about it, okay, honey?

Eric: Baby, you have to send the $971 to the security company, and I will plead with them to proceed with the delivery, okay? This is the address the security company gave to me this morning. That is what you are going to use in sending the money to them, okay, baby?

Jenna: Okay, how do I do that?

Eric: Baby, I am going to give you the address that the company gave to me an hour ago, okay, honey?

Eric: The name is Israel. Go to Western Union or MoneyGram. Baby, are you there with me?

Jenna: Yeah, I will have to send it tonight. It is 10:00 a.m. I will have to go in the afternoon.

Eric: Yes, honey, can you do it in the afternoon or even now, if possible? I want the company to receive it today so they will proceed with the delivery, okay, honey? Baby, are you there with me?

Jenna: Yes, babe, I will go now and try it.

Eric: All right, baby. Let me know when you are done with it, okay, honey?

Jenna: Okay, I need to wait until 11:30 a.m., and I can only do $951. I need money in there to keep the account open. So it should be enough in Ghana money.

Eric: It's okay, baby. Honey, when you are sending it, take a clear picture of the transfer slip and send it to me so I can keep record of it, okay? And then you will also forward it to the company. I miss you very much, honey.

Jenna: Can you forward it to the company as I only have thirty minutes?

Eric: Okay, I will do that. You are going to send me your home
     address and phone number. I will forward everything to the
     company. Baby, are you going now?
Jenna: I'm here now.
Eric: Okay, baby. Let me know when you are done with it, okay,
     honey?
Jenna: Is Israel the last name?
Eric: No, it's the first name, okay, honey? Please check it very well so
     you don't make a mistake on it, okay, honey?
Jenna: They will receive $400 out of the $971 that I give them.
Eric: Are you done sending it?
Jenna: No, I'm in line.
Eric: Okay, honey. Let me know when you are done with it, okay,
     honey? It's his first name, honey.
Jenna: Thank you, God.
Eric: Why do you say that, honey?

Jenna sent the receipts after Jenna took a picture of them and
sent it to Eric.

Eric: All right, baby. I am forwarding it to the company right now,
     okay, honey? I will text you back shortly, okay, love? Honey, you
     made a mistake. I am already back to work. I will have to go
     back over there after work.
Jenna: They messed up my last name. I had to call for that as well. Is
     that a *U* or *V* in the last name?
Eric: It was supposed to be a *V*, not a *U*.
Jenna: UGH.
Eric: Yes, honey?
Jenna: My heard hurts. I'm sorry. It looked like a *U*.
Eric: Honey, you have to call them to change it right now, okay?
Jenna: I can't call. I am back at work. They already printed up the
     receipt. I will need to have them void this one, and I have to
     call again and get in line again. Hopefully, they don't take the
     money out twice.

March 29, 2018

Eric: Honey, yes, you can call them, and they will correct the name through their computer system, okay, honey? Baby, do you understand me?

Jenna: Done.

Eric: Okay, honey. I will let you know what the company says, okay baby? Thank you so much, honey.

Jenna: You are welcome.

Eric: Honey, I have sent it to the company, but they are requesting for your home address and your phone number, okay? I am going to forward it to the company. Oh, honey, how is work going?

Jenna: Grueling, and I woke up with a headache that is not going away. How was your day? It is almost night here.

Jenna: Thank you for the song you sent. I pray you get your box.

Jenna: Israel picked up the money. Hopefully, we won't have to do this again.

Eric: I hope so, my love. [Eric knew he would be asking for more as soon as Jenna got paid again.] I love you so much, honey. Honey, has the company gotten back to you? I love you so much. Text me when you get home.

Jenna: Yes, I am at work. Hopefully, you can get your box now.

Eric: Yes, my love, and thank you so much, honey. My heart is at rest now, my love. Text me when you get home.

Jenna: You are welcome, and I am glad I could help you. I will text you. It is 4:34 p.m., and I am leaving at 6:00 p.m., an hour and a half more.

Eric: Okay, honey. I will be waiting for you, my love.

Jenna: Thank you for my song.

Eric: You are always welcome, baby.

Jenna: So your birthday is on July 17, 1964?

Eric: Yes, my love, and I am praying I am out of here before then so we will celebrate it together, okay, honey?

Jenna: I pray that you are out too.

Eric: Oh yes, my love. You remembered very well, honey. I really want to celebrate it with you.

Jenna: Sounds good. I will be fifty-six before you turn fifty-four.

Eric: Hello, baby. Are you still at work? I miss you so very much, honey. Good night and sweet dreams to you, my love. I will text you in the morning before going out on patrol. Kisses and hugs to you, my sweet love.

Jenna: Sorry. I had a call from my brother. My father is in the hospital, and he is out now. I just called him. 'Night, sweetheart. I hope your sleep is tranquil, and I hope your dreams are bright. I miss talking to you.

Eric: I miss talking to you, my love, and I missed you the whole night, my sweet baby. Honey, am sorry about your dad. I am praying for him. I hope he is good now, my love.

March 30, 2018

Eric: Good morning to you, my love. I keep thanking God for bringing an angel like you into my life, and you are a blessing to me, baby. My heart, my whole body, and my soul choose you because you are the other half of me. You were created for me, and I was created for you. I keep staring at your picture and wondering about what I have done without you. Thinking of you is the most wonderful thing I have done in my whole life. My memories of you keep ringing in my head and heart every second of my life. I can't wait to look you straight in the eye and ask you to marry me. I can't wait to travel on vacation with you, honey. I can't wait to be the only one to kiss you good morning, sweetheart. I love you so much, honey.

Jenna: Good morning, or what time is it there? The dog needed to go out, so I got up with him. But I can't go back to sleep. I love you and can't wait to meet you.

Eric: Wow, that is cool, honey. How was your night? I hope you slept well, my sweet baby. I am going out on patrol, okay, honey?

Jenna: Yes, I slept until Milo woke me up. Happy Good Friday.

Eric: Oh, thank you so much, baby. I wish was there to celebrate with you, my love. How is your dad? I hope your day is going well.

Eric: I just want you to know that I am always here, loving and missing you so much, my love.

Eric: Kisses and hugs to you, my sweet baby. Text me when you are free.

Jenna: Okay, I am at work. I feel like this can be a long day, ugh. There is something wrong with my connection. I hope you are okay. I never paid my phone bill, so I can't text you. [Jenna was so concerned for Eric and his box that she wasn't paying any of my bills.]

Eric: I'm okay, honey, and I have missed you so much. Honey, text me when you get time. I will definitely wait for you tonight, okay, love?

Jenna: Yeah, he is a good kid. He knows I am good for it. [Jenna's son paid her phone bill, and she paid him back. Her son had no idea that she was giving her money away.]

Eric: Wow, that is cool, baby.

Jenna: Yeah, he is a good kid, he knows I am good for it. Have you eaten?

Eric: Yes, my love, and I am waiting to hear from the woman whom I cherish so much. And that is you, honey.

Eric: Honey, have you heard from the company?

Jenna: Awww, you make me smile.

Eric: Thank you so much for saving my box, my love. I'm glad I made you smile, honey, and I will do, my love.

Jenna: You are welcome. My phone was off, so no, not yet.

Eric: All right, baby. I will send your details to them, and they will get back to you soon, okay, love?

Jenna: What is your favorite food, and how do you like your coffee?

Eric: Honey, I love any food that is prepared by my woman, and I like a brown coffee without sugar, honey. I hope you are going to cook for me when we are together. I really don't have a favorite meal that my wife makes for me.

Jenna: I love to cook. I haven't had a chance to. As long as you take me out once in a while, I will cook for you. XOXO. I also love lobster, steamers, and corn on the cob. I cook lasagna, chicken parmesan, chicken Kiev, chicken soup, and turkey, and I drink my coffee black, with no sugar.

Eric: Wow, that is cool, honey, but I am not planning to marry you because you are already my wife. Sorry for the late reply, okay, baby? I went to have a few words with the soldiers.

Jenna: LOL. It doesn't work that way, babe. The next time I commit to a man, I want it in writing. Actions speak louder than words.

Jenna: First, courtship, then boyfriend, and then an engagement ring. The man will be still head over heels like it will be, then the marriage and the piece of paper that shows that I am worthy.

Eric: Baby, I assure you I am working on it, and I know you have been hurt before. And I want you to know I am not perfect, but I promise to always make you happy. I know God is going to protect this relationship and that we will be happy forever.

Jenna: My brother had a beach ceremony in Aruba. They called me Jenna Razzie.

Eric: Baby, can you send me one of the pictures?

Jenna: I am not perfect either. When I have someone that I love, they certainly know it. I have only fallen in love three times. Each time ended horribly, and I walked away.

Eric: Wow, awesome, and I want you to know I will always love you. Baby, you are ready with your man when you get married. I want you know that I will always love you, and I know God will lead us on the right path.

Jenna: Ready, huh? Yes, God will.

Eric: Yeah, that's cool, baby. I have a four-bedroom apartment in Florida, and it's gonna be lovely spending the rest of my life with you, baby.

Eric: I know you won't know how serious I am until you see me face-to-face. I love you with all my heart, and everything about me keeps singing your name.

Jenna: You make me smile.

Eric: I am glad I do, baby. Honey, are you still at work?

Eric: Honey, are you still there with me? 😣 😣 😣 Honey, I just received an email from the security company.

Jenna: Oh no! What now!

Eric: Honey, I am dead. Look what the email company just sent.

Eric: Honey, the company emailed me that everything is going well but that they have one more document to finalize called power of attorney, which must be done. It is an agreement between Ghanaian UN and the US government. They say that without the document, the delivery cannot take place. So I asked them now much the document will cost, and they said they want 16,200, which we should be fast with.

Jenna: I don't have that, sorry. [At this point, Jenna was sick to her stomach, thinking about all this money and how to get him out of the situation. She had no idea that he was romance-scamming her, and she felt like throwing up.] Power of attorney for what? [Jenna learned later that the package box he wanted her to pick up probably had drugs in it.]

Eric: 😩😩😩 Baby, is there no way you can help me? I promise I am going to pay you back double. Please, honey, please.

Jenna: Not with that kind of money. Can't you get a loan?

Eric: Honey, you know I can't do anything like that from here, I swear on my honor. I should have had him, I swear on the Bible. [His honor meant nothing.] I am going to pay you back. [Eric promised this throughout the eight months that they talked, and he never paid Jenna back, not even one penny.]

Jenna: No, I don't have the credit or the means to do that. I am not going to take out any more savings. I don't know why they reneged on the promise. I am not rich, and I can't afford to pay anymore. I want to help you out, but there seems to be something off with the company. [At this point, Jenna knew there was something off, but she thought that the company was the one that was the scammer, not Eric.]

Eric: Honey, I swear on my honor I am going to pay you back everything as soon as my box is delivered to you. I will give you the code to open it so you can take back the money you spent in receiving it, with interest. Baby, I promise to pay you back double. I need you the most. I don't have anyone else to turn to. Honey, please. 😩😩😩

Jenna: I don't know what else to do for you. You are asking me to get money I don't have. I took a loan last year on my Fidelity account. I can't take any more. I am paying it back with interest. This seems a little shady from where I am looking at it. I gave you money for Jerry. That was great. I still owe $1,100 in taxes. I am sorry. I haven't even met you yet. I don't know what to do for you. [Jenna should have walked away from this, but she was already invested in the connection and didn't want to seem selfish.]

Jenna: The money that I have left is all the money that I have for my kids when I die, and I am not touching that.

Eric: But, baby, I will pay you back, and I am going to replace it with interest. And I know you have not seen me, but believe me. I really need this money when I retire. Please, honey, please. You know my box will be with you until am out of here.

Eric: Baby, are you there with me? Honey, please don't leave me 😢 😢 😢 [It's always the crying emoji.]

Jenna: I can't get it out without paying a 10 percent penalty. For all I know, you could be kids posting a handsome man's picture on here. [Bingo. That is exactly what was happening.] For all I know this handsome man doesn't even know someone is using his face [which is exactly what was going on]. I have never come across anything like this before. I don't know what to think. I am sorry for thinking this way, but if you were in my shoes, you would think the same way. I am sure of it.

Eric: Honey, I am not going to be angry cause I know who I am, and I understand how you feel. But I want you to know I will always love you, and I can never pretend to be who I am not. Honey, this money is my life savings and all I have labored for. I promise to pay you back. You're going to take the money you spent in receiving it when it is delivered, okay, hon?

Jenna: I don't have 16,000 to give you. How much in American dollars?

Eric: Honey, that is $16,200, okay, baby? Baby, are you still there?

Jenna: I don't have $16,000 to give. If I hit the lottery, I would gladly give it to you.

Eric: Oh my god. 😰 😰 😰

Eric: Honey, you aren't going to be happy if I lose such an amount of money for our future. We both need this money for our future when I am finally out of here. Right now my eyes are filled with tears. Honey, please. Oh my god. Baby, are you there with me?

Jenna: I am with you. I can't get that much money, I am sorry. I would if I could.

Eric: It's okay, baby. Let me lose my box. 😰 😰 😰 Let me lose everything I have labored for, baby. You are the only hope I have. Please don't turn your back on me.

Jenna: I am not turning my back on you, but this is a little too much for me to handle I don't know how to help you.

Eric: I guess you are sleeping already. I will text you later. I am not going on patrol because my head hurts because of this, baby. I believe I am about to lose such an amount of money, honey.

Eric: Good night. Sweet dreams.

March 31, 2018

Jenna: If you have all this money, then why don't you have the people take the $16,200 out of your box to pay for it?

Eric: If I could work it out that way, do you think I would seek your help? That's their rules over here. They don't touch your money until it is delivered to you, okay, honey? I told you I will pay you back with interest. I have not been myself ever since I received the email from the security company. I am going to lose all that I have labored for. Honey, will you be happy when we're finally together and I tell you I lost my millions of dollars because of $16,200? I know it's a lot of money for you. Honey, help me. If you really loved me, you would help me. [They play with your emotions. They had no intention of paying Jenna back at all, and she didn't know who she was talking to for eight months.]

Eric: Please, honey, I promise to never let you down.

* * * * *

Well, I am halfway living out of my car. The other car was repossessed, and I am grateful that I am living with my family and have a roof over my head, food to eat, and clothes on my back. But I would have my car and an apartment with my son if I did not help this man, who promised time and time again that he would help me. It was my wrongdoing, and I am the one to blame for my actions. But my heart got the best of me, and I will never ever do this again. If you are in this situation now, please, I beg of you, do not send a cent to these people.

* * * * *

Eric: I love you so much, honey. You are the reason behind my smile. Thoughts of you keep me going here, my love, and I will never do anything to hurt your feelings, okay, honey? Good morning to you, my love. I love you so much. Nothing is gonna change that, honey.

Eric: I have been crying all night, baby, please help me, honey.

Eric: Hello, baby. Are you still sleeping? Honey, please help me out. You know I don't have much time left, my love. You will take back that money as soon as my box is delivered to you. It is not going to take twenty-four hours. I beg you, my love.

I sent an email to see if I could help Eric in any way I could.

To whom it may concern,

I am sending this message on behalf of Eric Q. He is in the army and cannot get to his box. I am helping this businessman who does not want to lose his fortune. I am getting money up for him, but it will take three to six business days.

Respectfully yours,
Jenna R.

Hello, Jenna,

> We do not have much time left, so we advise you to make a payment on time. The box will be delivered to you without delay.
> Thank you. Hope to hear from you soon.

Jenna: How much time are we talking? We have already paid four thousand in African Ghana money.

Eric: Baby, it is not just a briefcase, okay? It's about the millions in it, and they said this document is very important, okay, honey? Please, my love. This is taking too much time, my love.

Eric: Honey, they said that if that document is not endorsed, then they can't risk delivering my box to you because it is going to be a risk for them, and they can be arrested, honey. So if they can get that document done, then nothing can hold them on their way, okay, honey? And it will be safe. I have some pieces of gold inside the box, honey. It's not just an ordinary briefcase, okay, honey? Honey, I am really going to give you 30 percent of the money. All I want is for my valuables to be safe with you, okay, honey?

Eric: Please, I will definitely pay you back double. I have not been myself ever since I received the email from the security company.

Jenna: I can't do anything now. It is the weekend, and it is not open. I have to wait until Monday. I need to think on this. I do not want to be arrested.

Jenna: I don't mind signing for you, but I can't come up with $16,200. This is making me sick!

Eric: Babe, I understand, and you are not going to be arrested. Trust your man, okay, honey? You know I won't allow you to get involved in anything that will hurt you, okay? Honey, I love you so much, and I will never do anything to hurt you, okay, my love? You are the only woman that gives me joy. You are the only women my heart beats for.

Jenna: They just called me.

Eric: What did they say?

Jenna: The connection was lost. I can't call them back.
Eric: Maybe it's the signal, honey, and what do they say to you, my
      wife?
Jenna: They asked if I was the person that they were delivering the
      box to, and I said yes. And the connection was lost.
Eric: Baby, that's to tell you how serious this is, and you know they
      will be forwarding it at any moment. Honey, has the company
      replied to you after you emailed them?

Jenna sent the e mail that was sent to her.

> To whom it may concern,
>
> Where did the four thousand dollars in
> Ghana money go? Shouldn't have this amount
> gone to the 16,200? Sorry, I am just trying to get
> this all straight.

And this is what was sent back.

> I am Mr. O. P. Saboo.
> Hello, madam. We understand what you are
> talking about, and we have processed all the nec-
> essary documents to get the box out of the com-
> pany. The certificate called the power of attorney,
> which costs $16,200, madam, is very import-
> ant. It is a noninspector agreement between the
> Ghanaian government and the United States gov-
> ernment, needed in all deliveries of goods, and it
> also prevents the police from inspecting the box.
> Madam, this is very important. We have to get
> it done on time to enable the delivery process to
> continue its progression. I hope to hear from you
> soon. [They never answered my question; they
> only played on the fear of losing the box.]

Jenna: Eric, I can't do anything over the weekend. Why do you have to pay so much? Why don't they want the government to look in your briefcase? I don't want to be carrying illegal stuff. This is not sitting right with me. I don't want you to lose your fortune, but I don't look good in orange. And that is what the color is for jail. UGH.

Eric: Baby, if this is going to cost you any harm, I would not have allowed you to help me get my box, okay, honey? It's my stuff, and the Ghanaian government needs to sign the agreement. The document is to ensure my box is going to be delivered to you safely, okay, honey? I told you it was a crude-oil-and-gold business, and that tells you it was a legit business. I would never get you involved in illegal stuff, okay, honey? I will never get you involved in anything that will hurt you, okay, my love? Baby, stop thinking about jail, okay? Everything will be fine as soon as my box is delivered to you, okay, my love?

Eric: I have missed you so much, honey. You know you always make me smile with great joy with your sweet words, and I have missed those words so much. I have missed all our sweet and lovely words. Honey, are you still at work?

Jenna: Yeah, I am still working. I wish you were here with me, going through this. Then you could go and get a check. Don't you have any money in the book?

Jenna: You could take some of your 401(k) or 403(b), couldn't you?

Eric: Baby, if was there with you, I wouldn't bother you about it because I could pay the amount to get my box, but don't worry. We are going to be together soon, and we are going to be smiling while talking about what we went through together, my love.

Jenna: So you couldn't have your bank send the money to them?

Eric: Honey, I'd have to be present myself at the bank to do that because I froze my account before going on this mission for security reasons. And it's also because my account has been hacked before. To avoid things, I have frozen the account until I am back at the States, and I have to go to the bank myself and activate the account before I can operate it, okay, honey?

If I could access my account through here, we wouldn't be going through this. I would have sent you the money from my account so you could send it to the company, and we wouldn't be going through this right now.

Jenna: Ahhhhh.

Eric: Honey, text me when you get home, okay? I love you so much. I miss you. honey.

Jenna: Hello, sweetheart.

Eric: Hello, baby. How was work today?

Jenna: Happy almost Easter.

Eric: Yes, it is already Easter here. Happy Easter to you as well. Baby, what are your wishes for Easter?

Jenna: Just that everyone will be happy and healthy, that my son will become the man I know he is made of, that my other son will find a job, for me to get out of debt, and for my sister to get some help. I pray for a new job. I pray for honest people that don't stab me in the back. I pray for the troops to come home and for all of you to be safe. I pray to have a house by the ocean where I can run on the beach barefoot. I pray for my true love to show me who he is and for the man that wants me and me alone. I pray for my own place and my own bathroom, which I can share with my family and my special someone. What are your wishes?

Eric: Wow, cool, and God is going to answer all your prayers, baby. Amen.

Eric: Honey, I pray to get out of here soon. I pray for God to always guide and protect my son. I pray to be the only one who kisses you good night and also good morning. I pray that God will guide and protect my future wife. I pray I am always happy with you. I pray we get married and spend the rest of our lives together. I pray my box gets to you safely. I pray nothing bad comes between us, and I pray to be forever happy with you, my love.

Jenna: Awww, that is so nice.

Jenna: You know, my friend from the neighborhood and I used to get a card for each other at Christmastime, and in that card, we would write who we chose to get a present for in honor of each other. She was my best friend and a neighbor. She asked me what I wanted to have as a present for a child who needed it.

Jenna: She and I did that every year after. She moved to Seattle last year, but that was one of the most treasured gifts along with the drawings, paintings, and letters that were written to me from people, friends, and family.

Eric: Wow, baby. That is nice. You make me smile with tears.

Jenna: Last year I volunteered to send Christmas stockings to the troops. I wish I knew you then. I am so sorry you are having a rough time. I wish things were better for you.

Jenna: I have given so much money to people, like my son. He always wants to pay me back, but I don't expect him to. The amount that they are asking for is too huge for me to wrap my head around. I am having a hard time with this, and I pray that after we send them this money, they won't turn around and say, "Now I want more."

Eric: I'm glad I do, my love. My heart has been empty for so long, and now that I realize what it takes to be happy, I don't wanna lose it. You gave me reasons to love again, reasons for me to smile again, reasons that make me believe I can't die here, reasons that makes me believe I still have a good life ahead of me, and reasons for me to call you my sweet wife. And I have missed all this for so long, baby. Thank you so much for making me who I am today, my love. I am proud to say I love you with all my heart, and I can't live without you, honey. I love you forever, my sweet wife.

Eric: Honey, they assured me that there will be no more money after this, and I promise there won't be any more money needed.

Jenna: You touched my heart with your words, and I really want to believe that you and I will see each other. I want you to be a real man who makes a promise to me and keeps it. I want to believe so much that you will still be with me after I give you all this money. It is hard for me because of all the lies I have been through with guys in the past, and I don't want to dwell on that with you. But this is just too far-fetched for me to wrap my head around because $16,200 is so-friggin'-much money to me. I know you have to spend money to make money. I want true love more than I would like money, but I would like to live comfortably with money. And I would like to know that my children would be comfortable as well. My soul has been searching for someone like you for so long.

Jenna: I have been in a relationship before that I thought would work out, then didn't. Every time I would give, give, and give, they would take, take, and take. I didn't ask for anything, but it always comes down to me being disappointed. I have been dreaming of someone like you for so long and that handsome face. I am going to jump in your arms and cry happy tears.

Eric: Baby, I am not perfect, but I keep praying to God to always guide us on the right path. Honey, I will do all my best to always make you happy. If not for my box, I wouldn't want your money, honey. I am okay with the feelings I feel for you in my heart, and I know we are going to make the world a better place for us. Believe me when I say I love you. Life has been so difficult for me, living alone these past few years. Now meeting you was the best thing that has ever happened to me. I know we have not met face-to-face, but what I feel for you right now is that you are more than a girlfriend to me, honey. The feelings I have for you are feelings of a soulmate, honey, and I can't wait to be with you for the rest of my life.

Jenna: I have to stop dwelling on the negative and start focusing on the positive.

Jenna: I do feel the same way. I believe our souls have been speaking to each other for years. [They never spoke, just texted.] I was just about ready to give up on love and be content on my own by myself, and you popped up on my Facebook screen. God, you are yummy.

Eric: Honey, I know you have been hurt so many times, and there is a saying that we always meet the wrong ones in life because when we finally meet the right one, we will be grateful for that gift. Honey, trust and belief is the key to a successful relationship, and we have to put all our past behind us and embrace what the future has for us. My heart melts for you sweet words, honey. You complete me, baby, and I love you so very much.

Eric: Words can't explain what I feel for you, honey. I want you to know that you will be in my heart forever. [This was probably said to fifty other women in the same day by him.]

Eric: What are your activities for today?

Jenna: I am working, then going to my brother, my nephew, and my sister-in-law's house.

Jenna: Thank you, God, for bringing Eric into my life. Thank you for having us meet this way. Please guide him and protect him from harm and on his journey. Please let him be safe, and please let us meet one day. For he is chipping away at my cynical heart, and he is my angel [Boy, did he have her fooled.]

Eric: Oh, thank you so much for the prayer, honey, and I know God will never forsake us. I believe in him, and I know he has something marvelous for both of us. Baby, what are your activities today?

Jenna: I am working.

Then Jenna sent Eric some YouTube music.

Eric: Baby, I am going to listen to the music when I get back from patrol. I have to rest right now, honey.

Jenna: I wonder what you are doing now. I used to sing in a choir. I was a cantor. I don't have a professional voice, but I can hold a tune. LOL.

Eric: I am going to listen to that one while sleeping, honey.

Eric: Wow, that is cool, babe.

Jenna: Good night. Sweet dreams.

Eric: We are going to sing together when we are together, and I don't have a very nice voice too. LOL!

Eric: I will text you before going out on patrol, when I wake up, honey. Good night and sweet dreams to you, my love.

Jenna: I am not going to sleep. I thought you were.

Eric: Yes, I have to rest for a short while, okay, honey? I have so many duties to execute today, my love.

Jenna: Oh, okay. I will let you go to your duties. I will be dreaming of you tonight. I used to sing the whole mass by myself. I sang for my friend's wedding.

Eric: Wow, that is sweet, my love, and I can't wait to sit beside you as you sing with your lovely voice. Night-night, my love.

Jenna: Good night. I can't wait to hear your voice.

Jenna: How is it that I have never heard your voice, touched your face, or held your hand but think about you all the time? I love you too very much.

I sent a picture of myself in a workout suit.

Eric: Wow, you look sweet, babe. Good morning to you, my sweet wife. How was your night? And I hope you slept well, my sweet wife.

Eric: Baby, I love you so much. I keep picturing your face each time I close my eyes. I know I will be with you very soon, my love. I can't wait to bring you breakfast in bed, honey. I can't wait to be the only man to sit at home, prepare dinner, and wait for you to come home every evening, honey. I wanna always be there for you anytime you need me, my love. I love you so much, sweetheart.

Jenna: Happy Easter, my love. I know that Easter is over now for you, and you are probably asleep. Just know that wherever you are, I am thinking of you.

Jenna: I wonder where you are right now. I pray that you are safe.

April 1, 2018

Eric: Hello, love. I am here now. I am sorry for not replying to you on time, okay, honey? I was so busy, and I had a rough and bad day today. But thank God I am alive.

Eric: I missed you so very much, honey.

Eric: Happy Easter to you once again, my love. I wish was there to celebrate with you. We would both go out for dinner, and then I would propose to you, my love. I can't wait to do that, my sweet wife. I can't wait to tell the whole world how wonderful you are, my sweet wife. I miss you so much.

Jenna: I miss you too. XOXO. I will text you. I am glad you are okay, and I prayed that you would be safe.

Eric: Yes, I am safe, my sweet wife. How was your day? I miss you so much, honey.

Jenna: Good. I am with my family. I have to go into work soon.

Eric: Oh, okay, honey. Honey, you have to send an email to the company so they will give you the details that you are going to use in sending the money to them, okay baby?

Jenna: Okay.

Eric: I wish I was there to celebrate with you, my sweet wife. Honey, I promise we are going to be together very soon, okay?

Jenna: Okay.

Eric: I can't wait to put a ring on your finger and ask you this question. "Will you marry me?"

Eric: I would be the happiest man on earth when that day comes, honey. How is your family doing today?

Jenna: Sorry, my phone died on the way to work, and I didn't have my charger with me. I needed to charge it first when I got home.

Eric: Okay, honey. Have you contacted the company? I will be waiting here for you.

Jenna: It's 53 percent here now.

Eric: Oh, good. I hope you had a great time with them, baby.

Jenna: I haven't seen my Gmail. I was looking for the email when my phone died.

Eric: Do you still have the company link with you?

Jenna: They are good. I love my brother, his wife, and my nephews.

Eric: Wow, that is cool, honey. I wish I was there with you, my love. I really miss you so very much, honey.

Eric: Honey, you have to contact the company so they will give you the address. I want my box to be delivered to you on time. Honey, are you there with me?

Jenna: I pray you are the man in this picture. I hope this is not a hoax. Your face melted my heartstrings. I am going to be very disappointed if I give you money and you are someone else that posted a picture of a nice working man. I will be devastated if you disappear after you get this money.

Jenna: Forgive me for thinking that way. I just hope and pray you are for real.

Eric: It's okay. I understand how you feel, and I would feel the same if I were you. I want you to believe in me. I want you to forget your old memories, and let's face the future together. I can't pretend to be someone I am not, and I will never joke with your feelings, okay? I love you and cherish you.

Jenna: Okay, babe. I am going to trust you completely because I have been asking for a man like you all my life. I have been asking to get out of debt and move to a better place, preferably somewhere warm by the ocean. God picked you for me, and I have to trust in him.

Eric: Thank you, honey. I swear on my honor that I will always make you happy.

Jenna: I don't know if I can get that much money.

Eric: Honey, I want you to contact the company so they will give you details that you are going to use in sending the money to them, okay? I don't want any delays in the delivery this time, okay, my love?

Eric: Tell them you wanna use it for a project or something, my love, okay? Honey, do you understand me? Are you with me?

Jenna: I contacted them. My phone had a virus, and someone tried to hack me. So I have been cleaning and using virus protection. I can't believe the pressure that they are putting on me. If I didn't have the money at all, they would be shit out of luck. Grrrrr.

Jenna: I am not doing it through Western Union, that is for damn sure.

Eric: Okay, I don't think so either. Can you get the money out tomorrow? Can you send money to the company? They are going to get back to you as soon as they receive your email, okay, honey?

Jenna: No, I don't think so. I have to go to Fidelity to see if it is even doable. Then I will get in touch with you.

* * * * *

I took money out of my Fidelity account to help him. I took all of it, and after my money dried up, I never heard from him again. It may also have to do with me calling the FBI on him.

* * * * *

Eric: Okay, honey, so what are you doing at the moment?

Jenna: Sitting, watching TV, and trying to get viruses off my phone, UGH. You said your day was horrible. Are you okay?

Eric: Honey, I lost a few of my soldiers yesterday, and I feel so guilty about their deaths. I wish there was something I could do to get all of them home. Things are getting worse here. I can't wait to hold you tight and kiss you all through the night, my love.

Jenna: Okay, sweetheart. I am sorry that you had to go through that, love. I can't wait for that day either.

Eric: We are going to be together soon.

Jenna: I wish I could give you a big hug and let you cry on my shoulder while you lay your head on my shoulder, and I would take your face, kiss you, hold you, and make you feel better.

Eric: My love, that's going to happen soon. I am sorry I dozed off, baby. My eyes are filled with sleep, my love. The time here is 7:00 a.m., and I have to go out on patrol by 9:00 a.m. I haven't slept, my love.

Jenna: Go to sleep, baby. You need your rest. XOXO.

Eric: Thank you so much, baby. I love you so much, honey. I will text you before going out on patrol, okay, honey? Kisses and hugs to you, my love.

Jenna: I love you too, babe.

Eric: I love you more, babe.

Jenna: I wonder what the compatibility that Gemini and Cancer has? July 17, 1964, and June 1, 1962.

Eric: Good morning to you, sweetheart. How was your night? And I hope you slept well.

Eric: Good morning to my most favorite person in the world. I wish you the sweetest day and the happiest moments. Know that I will miss you every moment that we are not together. Never forget that you mean the world to me, love.

Jenna: Good morning or afternoon to you. XOXO.

Eric: Hello, baby. How is your day going? I love you so much, baby.

Jenna: XOXO.

Eric: Honey, where have you been the whole day? Love, what is going on?

Jenna: Hi. Yes, I'm at work. It's a crazy busy day. I'm doing testing. Sorry, my phone is acting up. I'm not able to get into apps.

Eric: So how are you doing now, my love? Text me when you get home, okay?

Jenna: Hi. I just drove my friend Carol home. Now I am back at work. It is 6:49 p.m. here. What time is it there?

Eric: Honey, were you able to take the money out right now? Honey, talk to me. You know we don't have much time before the company folds with my money.

Eric: I keep thinking about you every second of my life, and I can't wait to be with you, honey. I can't wait to spend the rest of my life with you, honey. I love you so much.

Jenna: I am not sure how much you will love me now. I just called my investment company, and I had taken a loan out last year. So I can't take another one out until that one is paid off. I can't help you with the money.

Eric: Well, it's okay. I'll just have to lose my box. That's all. But you told me you had the money in your account, so why are you talking about an investment company again?

Jenna did not give him a response to that. The person will make you feel guilty, like it is your fault that they are losing something when they never had anything to begin with. Or they do have loads of money because they do this to very many people?

Eric: That won't change my love for you, okay? I already told you that you mean so much to me, and nothing is going to change that, okay, baby? It hurts me that I am gonna lose my box, all that I have labored for all my life.

Jenna: I don't have it in my bank. I was going to take it out of my Fidelity account, but because I have another loan already being paid off, I can no longer take any money out.

Eric: I have planned to use this money to build a private hospital or start up a big business, but I guess all my plans are in vain now.

Jenna: I am sorry. I would if I could. Why are they asking for so much? You can still do that when you get back. You are a hard worker. If I could do that for you, I would in a heartbeat. So what happens to the money we already put in? Will you at least get that back?

Eric: I know you have the money, but you just don't want to help me out. It's okay. Thank you so much, and let me lose my box, baby. It's a pity you don't feel for me like I feel for you, honey. If you were in my shoes, you would do anything in this world to support me and make me happy.

Jenna: I do want to help you out. I can't take another loan out until I pay off this one. If there were some way for me to help you, I would. What about a government agency?

Eric: What do you mean, government agency? Don't tell anyone about my box because I don't trust anyone. I trust you with my life, and that is why I'm seeking your help, okay, honey? Do you understand me? [At this point, Jenna should have gone to someone. Then she wouldn't have spent so much.]

Jenna: Okay, I do feel for you. I can't take the money out. They told me no. I am insulted that you would think that I don't feel for you. This isn't going to work between us if you think I am holding money from you. Maybe you need to find yourself a rich woman and forget about me!

Eric: You told me you had money you were saving for your son. So can't you take from it and send it to the company? You will get it back as soon as my box is delivered to you.

Jenna: I have helped you out twice now without any hesitation because I had the money to give to you. And I am sorry about your box, but I came in at the tail end of this situation. I don't want to be blamed for not having $16,200 when you needed it. That is not fair, and it is not right for you to say such things.

Eric: 😢 😢 😢 So I am going to lose my $2,200,000 just like that?

Jenna: That is the money. It is in a 403(b). I took the loan to try to get out of the house that I am in. My car died, and I had to get another car. I really can't afford the car payment. So half went to that, and half went to my son's car because his car had problems. I helped him out with the money, and by then, I didn't have a lot. I drained my other account for you, my Acorns account. Can't you call them and ask to unfreeze your account? I did my due diligence to get you what you needed. I am sick to my stomach about all of this, and there isn't anything I can do.

Eric: You know that won't be possible. My presence is needed, and I have to sign documents for it. Don't you have any friend who can loan you the money? We will pay them back as soon as you receive the money. This is too much heartbreak right now. 😢 😢 😢 [Those damn crying emojis.]

Jenna: I am sorry. You are priceless to me, but I can't take the money out until I pay the loan off.

Eric: What about the money you were saving for your son?

Jenna: I don't have any friends that I could ask for that kind of money, and I wouldn't do that. The money that I was saving for my sons was the money that I have already given you. That was half of our security deposit. I could have been in an apartment by now. I am starting from scratch again and will need to stay in the house longer now. 😢 😢 😢

Jenna: My Fidelity account is for when I die, and my boys will each get half of what is in there. I am sorry. I know you were counting on me to pull you through, and I would if I could. I paid $950 for you. I know you think that is small change, but it is everything I had.

Eric: So you are giving up on me. [At this point, Jenna should have blocked his ass. Now she wouldn't give him money at all.]

Jenna: I am not giving up on you. I love you but cannot come up with the money you need. Unfortunately, you did not pick a rich woman. I will be rich one day. But take me for who I am, or don't take me at all. Find another woman to pay for your box.

Eric: Baby, is there nothing we can use to get a loan at the moment?

Jenna: My credit sucks. They wouldn't give me a penny.

Eric: Baby, what about the white-gold ring? It is going to get up to that if you sell it. We are going to buy another one as soon as you receive my box.

Jenna: The white-gold ring only costs $700. I am sure it is not worth that now. I have had the inserts replaced where they fell out. The only one who thinks the ring is priceless is me because it belonged to my grandmother and grandfather. I will not sell my ring. I am at a loss. I don't know what to do.

Jenna: Seriously, is this what you do? Romance women, tell them what they want to hear, then find out what they own and take everything that they have? You give them a story about your kid losing his home and you losing your box from your company? Did you hack into my account to find out that I had an Acorns account? You seem to know how much I have in my accounts because that is exactly how much you need. Now I am scum under your fingernails because I can't get you what you want. SERIOUSLY? GRRRRR!

Eric: I guess losing my box will make you happy. [If Jenna could have bitch-slapped him, she would have.]

Jenna: No, it won't make me happy. Why would you say that?

Eric: Yes, it will. If not, you would have done something about it other than come up with stories. They have given me a deadline. This is the time I need you most. [It is all about them. They don't care about what you have gone through to try and get what they needed. If Jenna had been in a better state, she would have walked away from this con artist. Her mind was not in the right place.]

Jenna: I don't know what to do. You sound like a spoiled brat right now. You are in love with me when I am doing everything for you. When I fall short, you make me feel like shit. Thank you so much. I really appreciate that!

Eric: Losing it will not hurt you. That is the reason you are saying all of this. If you really wanted to help, you would.

Jenna: Tell me how to help you. Did you think of something?

Eric: You know what to do. If you really want to listen, if I lose my valuables, I will never be happy with you. You know that.

Jenna: Even if I had the money, which I don't, and if I did give it to you, I would never be happy because of the way you are making me feel right now. So I guess this is goodbye If I can find a way to get your money, I will, but you are right. It will never be the same for you and me.

Eric: Hi, baby. How are you doing? I miss you so much. [Seriously?] I have been thinking about you all day. [Again, seriously?] I have been dealing with the security company. They have agreed to help us out. We only have to pay $5,500. Baby, this is our only chance left. Baby, are you with me?

Jenna: That may be doable, but I need to see if I can take out that amount. Are they going to put the $950 as well?

Eric: Yes, honey, and then they will help us with the remaining balance. Please do all you can to come up with the money.

Jenna: I will see what I can do. I will need the information of where to send it if I can take the money out.

Eric: Honey, I will send an email to them, okay? I have missed you so much. Are you there with me?

Jenna: Sorry, I was on the phone with a recruiter.

Eric: So what is up, honey?

Jenna: I am working right now. The guy that I interviewed from the other job called me back.

Eric: Honey, the company just sent me the account details that you need to send the money to them, okay, baby? You have to send $4,600 and $900 through Western Union.

Jenna: I am not sure they can do it that way. I am taking it out of my Fidelity account.

Eric: Honey, don't fail me this time, okay?

Jenna: I will do everything I can, but I will not promise anything until I speak with them. I need to see if they can add on to the existing loan.

April 3, 2018

Eric: Can you call them so we can see what is up? Honey, these are the account details the company sent to me, and you are going to send $4,600 to them through this account, okay, honey?

Eric: The name is Marko, and here is the account number and the routing number. It will go to Wells Fargo, to a Steve R. in Georgia.

Jenna: Okay.

Eric: Honey, do you still have the other address with you, the one you used to send the $950 to the company?

Jenna: I think so.

Eric: Okay. You are going to use that same address to send the $900 to the company, okay, honey? What are you doing at the moment?

Jenna: An old boyfriend just called me on my work phone. I haven't talked to him in forever. I didn't even know who he was or his phone number.

Eric: An old what? Honey, what did you say? I hope he didn't try to talk to you funny. Honey, are you with me? Text me when you are free.

Jenna: Yeah, I'm driving.

Eric: All right, text me when you are free and drive safely. Hello, honey. Where are you? I miss you so much. Text me when you can.

Jenna: Okay. I went to the gym to work out.

Eric: Oh, nice, baby. So are you home now?

Jenna: Yeah, I just got home. My legs feel like spaghetti. LOL. I need to call tomorrow. By the time I got out of work tonight, it was too late.

Eric: Honey, you said your legs feel like spaghetti. Can I eat them? LOL.

Jenna: LOL. I don't think they will taste very good.

Eric: LOL. They will, honey. I miss you very much.

Jenna: Only if I can wrap my legs around that hunk of a body of yours. 😂😂😂

Eric: LOL. You made me laugh and happy. That is what I love about you.

Eric: It is still early in the morning here now. Honey, you told me about your old boyfriend that called you. What did he say?

Jenna: He called and asked what the code was for male implants. LMAO. I was caught off guard. I asked if he needed the diagnosis code or the procedure code. Then he started laughing out loud. He said his name, and I still didn't know who he was. Then I figured it out, and it was nice catching up with him. He likes to talk, and I do too. LOL.

Eric: Oh, I see. I have slept, my love. I was waiting to talk to you.

Jenna: Oh, you should get some sleep. I am sorry for keeping you up. You need your rest.

Eric: Thank you, honey. I usually love it when you tell me to go to sleep, baby. I love the way you pet me to sleep.

Eric: I love you so much, honey. I will text you before going on patrol, when I wake up, honey. Good night and sweet dreams to you, my love.

Jenna: Sweet dreams to you as well. XOXO. I will be dreaming of your beautiful cheekbones and eyes.

Eric: Thank you, honey, and I trust you with my life and my heart. Please don't hurt me, honey.

Jenna: I won't hurt you. I have given you my heart yesterday. I took part of it back with all that happened, so there is a wall up now. But I have no intention of hurting you. Let's get your box and then your money safely in the bank there for you. Then we can breathe again.

April 4, 2018

Eric: Good morning to you, my love. I hope you slept well. I wish was there to wake you up every morning by my side. I can't wait to go on a morning walk and an evening walk. I can't wait to travel on vacation with you, my love. When that day comes, I am going to be the happiest man on earth, baby. I love you so much, honey. I wish you a very wonderful day, baby, and I love you so much.

Jenna: Awww, thank you, babe. XOXO. How was your sleep? I wish you a wonderful day. You must be asleep. XOXO. Or are you on patrol? I just woke up.

Eric: I'm back from patrol, my love. Thank you for the song, my love. How are you doing? I miss you very, very much.

Jenna: Good. I just got into work, and I am hanging with my nephews tonight.

Eric: Oh, that's nice, baby. Honey, have you called to see how it goes?

Jenna: Not yet. I am going to call at 8:00 a.m. It isn't 8:00 a.m. yet.

Eric: Honey, please do all you can to get my box, okay? We don't have much time left, and this is the only chance we have left, honey.

Jenna: Okay. It is almost 8:00 a.m. I am putting in MIBIs and Lexiscans.

Eric: That's nice, baby, and have you eaten?

Jenna: No, not yet. How about you?

Eric: No, I haven't had my dinner, honey.

Jenna: I hope you will eat soon. I love the song that you sent. I am listening to it now.

Eric: I just wanna know what they say first, okay, honey? I am not hungry, honey. Honey, how is our son doing?

Jenna: Our son?

Eric: Yes, honey, or should I say *your son*?

Jenna: They are both good. How is Jerry doing?

Eric: No, honey, *our sons* because I can't be with their mother and still call them your sons now, okay, honey?

Jenna: Okay. That makes me smile. XOXO.

Eric: I'm glad I do, my love. Honey, I am going out on a brief meeting right now okay? I will text you when I am back.

Jenna: Okay, honey. I will text you soon, okay, love? Please be careful while you are on patrol. I just sent an email to see if I can add onto my loan.

Eric: Okay, what did they say, baby?

Jenna: Still working on it. Fidelity said no because I have a loan out, but I have another account. I'm not sure how much is in there. [Jenna told Eric that she had one more account that he could drain.]

Eric: Okay, baby. We really need to be fast about it, okay, honey? I don't wanna lose my valuables, baby. Honey, I am so weak and tired right now.

Jenna: I am sorry to add to your trouble.

Eric: Oh no, you didn't, okay, honey? I just want to rest for a short while, okay, honey? I will let you know.

Jenna: I am doing all I can think of to help you out. Unfortunately, you did not pick the right woman for finances. [Since this time, Jenna has studied *The Law of Attraction*, and at this point in her life, she was talking of lack in her life, not abundance. She needed to be grateful for what she did have in my life.]

Eric: LOL. Honey, you know am not doing that, and $2,200,00 is a lot of money to lose just like that, okay, honey? Think long-term. This money is going to take us, okay, my love? I wanna be all right with you, my love, and I have lots of plans for us. I will text you back soon, okay, my love? I love you so much.

Jenna: Okay. Hopefully, we can do something. Pray on it to get sleep, my love. Let me worry about it for now. XOXO. All set funds will be in my account in three to five business days.

Eric: I'm here now. I couldn't sleep. I was so worried.

Jenna: Please, dear God, help us get the money in time and help me give all that I have with the knowledge that this man will pay me back.

Eric: Honey, I swear on my honor to pay you back double, and I am a man of my word, okay, my love? Honey, how much was transferred into your account? [He had no honor, so swearing on his honor meant absolutely nothing.]

Jenna: You don't have to double it. Just pay me the money that I gave you so I can pay my taxes.

Eric: Oh, honey, I am going to surprise you, okay?

Jenna: LOL. [Yes, he surprised her, all right. Jenna found out the person she thought she was speaking to wasn't the person at all.]

Eric: Honey, can it be possible this week? I mean, will it be in your account on time so you can send it to the company this week? Honey, are you with me?

April 4, 2018
1:11 p.m.

Jenna: Hopefully, it will be by the end of the week.

Eric: Okay, honey. Now I can rest well because I have been so worried. Honey, are you busy at the moment?

Jenna: I am at work, feeling the fear, and doing it anyway. I pray you are for real.

Eric: Honey, you keep saying that, but it's okay because you are going to believe in me soon, okay? And I will never do anything to hurt you. I understand your fear, but I want you to believe in me. I love you so much, and I know you don't see that yet. But I pray to God that I get out of here soon so your fear will be over, honey.

Jenna: I do believe in you. That's why I took the money out. It is just that no one has ever said that to me before, and I am going to be incurring penalties for taking the money out. My taxes and car payments are overdue. It is all so overwhelming.

Eric: Honey, I will surprise you. Take my word for it, my love. Honey, what brand of car are you driving?

Jenna: A Nissan Sentra. It's not my first choice, but I didn't have much to choose from the Nissan dealer in Manchester, New Hampshire.

Eric: Honey, I am going to have a few words with the soldiers. I love you so much.

Jenna: Okay. XOXO.

Eric: Hello, baby. I am here now. Sorry it took so long, okay, honey?

Jenna: Hey, you. How are things there? I just made spaghetti for the boys.

Eric: Things are good here, my love. It's 2:31 a.m.

Jenna: Oh, wow, you must be tired.

Eric: How was work today?

Jenna: It was okay. I am looking forward to finding something else. I had a call from an entrepreneur. She used to be a lawyer and now stays at home with her kids and works for as long or as short as she wants to. And she is making money.

Eric: Honey, what do you mean, looking forward to finding something else?

Jenna: I had a phone interview and am waiting for a face-to-face.

Eric: OMG, my fingers and the keys are not compatible on this phone.

Eric: Wow, it's okay, honey.

Jenna: No worries. I am glad you are safe.

Eric: I am sorry for the late reply, honey. The signal is bad, my love.

Eric: It is okay. No worries. Honey, are you sure the money can and will be in your account by tomorrow?

Jenna: I am not sure. I am hoping I get paid, but I am way behind in my bills. I could possibly send a portion of it to them but not $900 with just my check.

Eric: I don't understand, honey.

Jenna: I get paid for my job tomorrow. The money I took out for you is from my mass mutual account, which I have been saving for almost two years. I took all that I could out. I kept enough to stop him keep the account open.

Eric: So you are going to send the $900 tomorrow?

Jenna: If the money is in there. I have to pay bills with my check.

Eric: Honey, I understand you have to pay bills, but send it to them tomorrow first, okay, honey? This is so they will know we are working on it.

Jenna: I am not sure how much my check will be. I may not clear $900.

Eric: Honey, you have to send something to them so they know we are working on it.

Jenna: I will send as much as I can. [FYI, never tell them when your check is coming or how much you have in your savings or other accounts. The more they know, the more they want, and they will not stop until they bleed you dry.]

Eric: Okay. Do all you can do, okay, honey?

Jenna: I will. Hey, you don't have all kinds of women sending you money, do you? 😆 😆 😆 LOL.

Eric: LOL. If I did, I wouldn't talk to you, okay? And please stop saying those words to me.

Jenna: LOL. Okay.

Eric: I love you so much. I don't need any other woman in my life, okay, my love?

Jenna: Just checking. You could be a great salesperson. I want you to know, and just so you know, I am not sending anyone money through here. 😆 😆 😆

Eric: I love you more than you'll ever know, honey.

Jenna: Awww, I love the song you sent me. I have never heard it before. Come to think of it, I have never given anyone that amount of money. I think you are worth it, though. [She was so wrong.]

Eric: Thank you, honey. I am going to pay you back, okay, love?

Jenna: More than money, I would love for you to be standing here in your uniform, picking me up.

Eric: I think that is the best thing that has ever happened to me, honey. I keep praying to God to guide and protect me till we meet face-to-face, and I have a lot of surprises for you, my love.

Jenna: Let me guess, giving me a big kiss and having my legs go weak? LOL.

Jenna: So are we buying a beach house, did I hear you say? 😆 😆 😆

Eric: Oh, I can't wait for that day to come, my love.

Jenna: It has to be by the ocean and not rocky. I like to run barefoot.

Eric: Wow, that is cool, baby.

Jenna: Will you run with me? I need music to run to keep in step with the beat.

Eric: Honey, whatever makes you happy. We will go on evening walks, and we will hold hands and talk about ourselves.

Jenna: I would love to hear about you. Where were you born?

Eric: Honey, I was born and raised in Orlando, Florida. Do you like traveling for vacation?

Jenna: You did tell me you were from Orlando, but I didn't know you were born there as well. I was born in Massachusetts.

Eric: Oh yes, I think I have been to Massachusetts once. I went to visit a friend there, but he is dead now. That was my first time, though, and it was fun. He didn't show me around, though.

Eric: What country would you like to go with me to on vacation when we first meet?

Jenna: I love walking in the beach hand in hand. I have only done that a couple of times with guys I have dated. Most guys I have dated didn't like the beach. I usually go by myself. I love that you love the beach.

Eric: I love the beach, especially ones with lots of sand, then I will race you and see who wins.

Jenna: I am sure you will win. I run, walk, and listen to music, and just being in the moment is priceless for me.

Eric: I love bringing coffee in the morning to my woman in bed.

Jenna: Will you go to the gym so I can watch those arms? LOL.

Eric: LOL. Yes, I do love the gym, baby. And yes, you will be on my back while I do my workout, honey.

Jenna: That made me giggle out loud. Are your eyes blue or green? It is hard to tell in this picture.

Eric: Shining blue. LOL.

Jenna: So what I know about you is that you were born in Orlando, Florida, you have a son named Jerry, you like your coffee with no sugar and just a little milk or black, you have huge, strong arms, piercing blue eyes, chiseled cheekbones, and a great smile, you are passionate, and you are a one-woman man. And from what you've told me, your voice is bass, and your birthday is July 17, 1964.

Eric: Baby, you said you love waking up in another way, so tell me about it.

Jenna: LOL. OMG, I am in trouble.

Eric: LOL. What trouble is that, my love? Honey, are you there?

Jenna: Yes, I just lost the connection.

Eric: Hello, baby? Are you there?

Jenna: Yes, I would love to wake up to you with good morning kisses all over. I need to keep it clean, but my mind is being dirty. LOL.

Eric: Cool, because I also thought of that, my love.

Jenna: You are in for a treat.

Eric: Oh yes, I can feel that, my love. I think it is time to think dirty, my love. So tell me, do you like it when a man sucks you?

Jenna: Depends what he is sucking on. LOL. The cheek? Nope. But the left breast? Hell yea. LOL.

Eric: Oh yes, that makes my head spin, baby.

Jenna: You will have more than your head spinning with this woman. LOL.

Eric: I love sucking my woman and making my woman scream.

Jenna: Mmmm, well, your head will not only spin, but it will also come off of your body. 😆 😆 😆

Eric: LOL. Cool, baby, and you will be whispering in my ears, honey. Honey, do you like long sex?

Jenna: Oh yes, but only with the right man. The longer the better.

Eric: Oh yes, baby, and I like to go all the way up.

Jenna: All the way up?

Eric: Oh yes, long after you say you are tired, my love.

Eric: Honey, what kind of movies do you like?

Jenna: I like murder mysteries, action-packed, comedy, or suspenseful.

April 5, 2018

Jenna saw Eric's text about vacation and answered him.

Jenna: I loved Aruba, but it wouldn't matter where we go as long as you are with me.

Jenna: I would take you to my mom's town, the beach, and a small bar with music. Then I would take you into Boston, the North End Faneuil Hall, the Freedom Trail, the Museum of Science, and the aquarium. Then I would take you to my favorite beach, Hampton Beach, and we would drive to Portsmouth and get a room with a hot tub. I would take you to dinner and to breakfast and look into your smoldering blue eyes, and I would think, *Jenna, you are the luckiest woman on earth.*

Jenna: It really doesn't matter where I am as long as I am with you. Newport in Rhode Island or sunny Florida, it doesn't matter to me as long as you are with me.

Eric: Thank you so much for the nice words. I love you more.

Eric: How was your night? I hope you slept well, my love.

Eric: I miss you so very much, honey, and I can't wait to be with you. You are the only woman whose name my heart keeps singing. I know I am not perfect, but I promise to always love you because that is what I know how to do best, baby. I can't wait to walk down the hills with you, my love. I can't wait to plan my life with you. I love you so much, baby. Honey, I'm going on patrol now.

Jenna: Okay. Be careful. I am going to rest. I hope you are okay.

Eric: Oh yes. I'm just coming back from patrol, my love. What are you doing?

Jenna: Driving.

Eric: Okay, baby. Be careful. Text me when you are free.

Jenna: my phone is not working great. It took me forever to send this message.

Eric: So what is up, my love? Baby, have you checked your account to see if the money is there? Honey, are you with me?

Jenna: Sorry. It was the charger that was not working. I could only send $200 today. It would have been better to wait for the check to come in.

Eric: No, honey, send $900 to them, then you can take it back when the check arrives. Do you understand me? Those are the instructions they gave me. Baby, where are you?

Jenna: Sorry. My phone wasn't working. I pulled the battery out, and I can text again. I am at work. Yes, I can give them $200 today, and when the check arrives, I can give them more.

Eric: No, honey, they said $900, not $200. I pray it arrives on time, my love, because we don't have much time left, okay?

Jenna: Okay.

Eric: Honey, are you still at work?

Jenna: I just left. I had a hard day at work and gave my two weeks' notice. I cannot stand the stress anymore. It has been awful for a month now. I have been trying to keep everything together. I know good things are coming, and I need to get a job fast.

Jenna: I have been here for almost three years. NEHI and St. Joseph's was wonderful to work for, but Manchester? Not so much.

Eric: I am sorry. I wish I was there to help you. I wish I could cuddle you through the night.

Jenna: I pray I get a job soon. I have an online thing I am interested in. My phone is not holding a charge.

Eric: Honey, have you checked to see if the money is in the account? I keep thinking of you, honey. I can't wait to be with you for the rest of my life.

Jenna: No, not yet, love.

April 6, 2018

Eric: Honey, I am sorry I nodded off. I was so weak and tired. I missed texting you last night, but I am feeling strong. I hope you are good, my love. I miss you so much, honey.

Eric: I asked God to send me the best girlfriend in the world. He sent me a wonderful woman who has become my true friend, passionate lover, and caring partner, and she is the one without whom I cannot live. I bless God for the day I found you.

Eric: Where are you, honey? I haven't heard from you the whole day. I feel worried, my love. Honey, what is going on?

Jenna: I was hacked on my phone. It wouldn't work. I tried to go to Hangouts but couldn't get the app. I finally figured out how to do it. If the money came in, I was just going to send the money to you.

Eric: Oh my god, baby. I have been so worried, my love.

Jenna: I have been worried about you too.

Eric: Honey, have you received the check now? It was like my heart left me. Please don't leave me like that again, baby.

Jenna: Not yet, but the bank just stopped my account. Someone took $4, then they tried to take $203. That's such a weird amount.

Eric: Who was that, my love? You said that the bank stopped your account? So how are you going to know if the money is in your account? Honey, you know this is taking too long.

Jenna: I am going to the bank tomorrow morning when it opens to get a new card and see about the money.

Eric: My heart was so sad the whole day, my love. I thought I lost you, honey.

Jenna: I wouldn't do that to you. That would be horrible karma. I didn't eat the whole day. I was worried about you.

Eric: Oh, thank God my wife is back. I am so happy.

Jenna: I am happy too.

Eric: What are you doing at the moment?

Jenna: Sitting with Milo, the dog I live with.

Eric: Wow, cool.

Jenna: You spoil me with your love songs. What are you doing?

Eric: I am sitting here with my desktop computer, waiting for my woman to text me, and here she is. I miss you too, honey, I am glad you like the songs.

Jenna: No, I am at home. Sorry for making more stress for you.

Eric: So what did you do the whole day?

Jenna: I worked. I was on the phone with the bank and worried about you.

Eric: How are our sons doing? You are the queen of my heart and the mistress of my fate. The best thing that happened to me was meeting you, my sweet woman.

Jenna: God, I missed you, my king.

Eric: I have always thought a person can experience happiness once in a lifetime, but with you, I realized that happiness for me is every minute and every second of every romantic day that I spend with you, which is remarkable. People say nothing good comes easy, but mine came to me in the easiest way. And that is you, my love. I can't stop thanking God for bringing you into my life. You gave my life meaning, honey. God bless you so much, my queen.

Jenna: The king of my heart. I love you. God brought you to me because he knew I needed love, and he made my wish come true. I hope you are not disappointed when you see me. That picture I sent was a long time ago, when I was forty-seven. I am fifty-five and have a lot more weight on me.

Eric: Oh, don't say that, my love. If I can love the old you, I can love the new you as well. It doesn't matter what you look like. It matters what I feel for you, and what I feel for you right now is unforgettable love. I love you so much.

Jenna: You are making my heart melt.

Eric: Baby, are you going to the bank in the morning?

Jenna: Yes, in the morning. Will I be sending it to the same guy I sent it to before? Except with a *V*, correct?

Eric: Yes, honey. How much will you be sending them?

Jenna: $900.

Eric: Okay, honey, and the other $4,600 should go into the account whose details the company gave me to send to you, okay, my love?

Jenna: Yes.

Eric: Okay, honey. I have to rest for a while because I have so many duties to execute today. Honey, please don't learn much that again, okay? Are you with me?

Jenna: Okay, sweetheart. Rest. Sweet dreams.

Eric: Okay, baby. I will text you when I go on patrol. Kisses and hugs.

Jenna: I love you. Where did you come from?

Eric: Honey, God made you for me and I for you, so I think we both came from God. LOL. 'Night, baby.

Jenna: 'Night, my love. May your sleep be peaceful, may your dreams be real, and may you feel me near you whenever you need me.

Jenna: While you were sleeping, I thought of you. I thought about flying on the astrological plane landing in your bed, crawling in beside you, wrapping my head on your masculine chest, and falling asleep in your arms. I am there with you in spirit. I trust you wholeheartedly with my money, soul, and heart. I know that you will never put me in harm's way and that you will protect me and keep me safe. I know you even though I have never met you. I truly trust in you.

Eric: Oh, thank you so much, honey. You make me smile big. Good morning to you, my love.

Eric: In my next lifetime, I will go through every storm and inclement weather to find you faster and spend every second of my life with you, my beloved. Only one thing would make me happy, which is to see your eyes every morning for at least fifty years. You are my life. I love you so much, honey. You are the answer to my prayers and the most beautiful gift given to me by the Lord. I love you from the bottom of my heart.

Eric: I told you God created you for me and I for you, my love. My love for you will last forever from the bottom of my heart.

Jenna: Okay, my love. Please be careful. I was sleeping. It is 5:00 a.m. right now. I am probably going back to sleep. Milo had to go out. XOXO. I will be at the bank soon.

Eric: Hello, baby. I'm back from patrol.

Jenna: I have the $900.

Eric: Okay, honey. Go send it to the company right now. Honey, what about the $4,600?

Jenna: I only cleared $5,200 after taxes were taken out. I may have to wait until Thursday to pay the rest. I am really late on my car payment because I have been helping you. And I want to help you, but this is pretty much draining my account.

Eric: No, honey, not $4,500. Okay, the whole payment was $5,500, and they said you should take $900 from it and send it through Western Union. That is going to leave you with $4,600, okay, my love?

Jenna: I gave the $900. I understand you I asked for $5,500. They took out taxes, so I only cleared $5,200. I gave $900. They are getting three thousand in Ghana money.

Eric: So how much is remaining with you, my love?

Jenna: I don't know. I have to go to the bank and see.

Eric: Okay. Thank you so much, baby.

Jenna: I have $4,379 left in the account. Please be for real. I have never ever done anything like this before. If I told anyone, they would think I have gone crazy. I am putting my full trust in you. I pray you are for real.

Eric: Honey, I told you not to worry yourself about that, okay?

Jenna: Okay.

Eric: Soon you are going to see me, and then you will be happy and trust me for life.

Jenna: Okay, sweetheart.

Eric: Honey, go and send the $4,379 to them first so they can proceed with the necessary endorsement and be ready to deliver my box to you, okay? Honey, take a picture of the transfer slip so I can forward it to them right now, okay?

Jenna: Do you still look like the picture in the photo? It is okay if you don't. I just want to be able to pick you out from the crowd.

Eric: LOL. I am still like that because I always do my workout every day to maintain my muscles, okay, my love?

Jenna: Mmmm, I can't wait to see them. I used to have awesome muscles, but I lost them.

Jenna sent a picture of the tracking number for Eric's friend to get the money.

Eric: Honey, I will text you in a few minutes.

Jenna: Okay. Do what you have to do. Can I leave $79 in so I don't close my account?

Eric: Okay, honey.

Jenna: How do I send it?

Eric: Honey, go to a Wells Fargo bank and make the deposit into the account whose details I sent you, okay?

Eric: Honey, can't you go there yourself?

Jenna: I am seeing where there is one.

Eric: Okay, my love.

Jenna: I talked to someone in Western Union. The quickest way to send funds is to pull up a cash app. That way, I can send it directly to you, and you can send it to the place. The closest Wells Fargo is three states over, in Bloomfield, Connecticut.

Eric: Hold on, babe. Let me contact the company. I will get back to you. [My guess is that he was contacting his wife or his partner that he lived with.

* * * * *

The more I type this and the more I read this, the more I can't believe that I was fooled to give all that I had away to someone that I had never ever met. My head was not in the right spot at all.

* * * *

Jenna: I don't know where there is a Wells Fargo around here. There is not one near me. The closest one is a hundred miles away.
Eric: Hold on, babe. Let me contact the company. I will get back to you.
Jenna: Okay, question, how can you call a company but can't call me?
Eric: Contact them through the email address.
Jenna: Okay, what is the email address?
Eric: You have it already. You have been contacting them, remember?
Jenna: I just contacted them to see if they will accept my payment, but I haven't heard back from them.
Eric: Okay, babe.
Jenna: I didn't give them any information yet. [At this point, Jenna was still thinking that the company was the scammer, not Eric.]
Eric: Okay, babe. Which bank is close to you? The company replied to me by asking me that. I will ask them to give me the bank details so that on Monday, you can go to deposit the money.
Jenna: Wasn't that your company? How do I do that? I get out after 4:00 p.m., and the bank closes at 4:00 p.m.
Eric: You can try. Just give it a try, my love, so that my box will get to you.
Jenna: I only have a half-hour lunch, and the bank is not near. I would have to punch out early?
Eric: Okay, my love. I will get details from them so that I can forward them to you, my love.
Jenna: How big is this box? And once I have it, do you want me to set it up in annuity or put it in the bank?
Eric: Thank you so much for your understanding, my love. Babe, you are going to keep it where you know it will be safe.

Jenna: I can bring it to Bankers Life. They wanted to hire me for insurance, but I couldn't pass the stupid test. I may go back and try again.

Eric: Okay, my love. Then you have to wait once the box is delivered to you, and we can plan on that. For now, let it be a secret between both of us.

Jenna: I will set it up as an annuity for you at Bankers Life.

Eric: Okay, babe. Babe, can I say something?

Jenna: Okay. I am not telling anyone about this. They will think I am crazy. I just pray this is real. Yes, go ahead and say something.

Eric: This is real. You know I will never let you down. I am happy to have you in my life, and I don't want to lose you. Without you I am empty. I want you always, my love.

Jenna: I don't want to lose you either.

Eric: You are my everlasting love. We will grow together, babe. You are my joy, babe. Nothing on earth can be compared to the love I have for you.

Jenna: I want that more than anything. I trust in you. I am not sure why because I haven't trusted a lot of people. I have been listening to the law of attraction, and I keep saying, "My money is in vibrational escrow." [The money was with Jenna physically. The law of attraction gave it to her. She decided to give it away to someone she did not know.]

Eric: Babe, everything is okay. It is fine.

Jenna: You know I will keep your money growing for you. This you can trust with me.

Eric: Babe, I trust you with my life. I know you will never let me down, babe.

Jenna: I trust you with my life as well.

Eric: Babe, to the world, you are nothing, but to me you rule the world. I want you in my life more than breath. [How did he know that to the world, she was nothing?]

Jenna: Wow, that is awesome. You make me smile. Just so you know, I do want you to breathe.

Eric: Babe, awesome cannot be compared to the beauty I see in you.

Jenna: Awww, I love you so much. I don't know how this happened. All this is from me seeing you in your uniform and that gorgeous smile, then seeing that body. God, thank you for bringing Eric into my life.

Jenna: If they can do a cash app, I can send the money right to them today. That is what the Wells Fargo person said.

Eric: Babe, they said they want it deposited into the account. I should be the one thanking God for bringing you into my life.

Jenna: What if I FedEx'd the check to Wells Fargo?

Eric: Babe, we should do it the way they want it, okay?

Jenna: Okay.

Jenna: I can't wait for the first time that I can kiss you. You must have fallen asleep.

Eric: I am here now, my love.

Jenna: Were you asleep? What time is it there?

Eric: I am sorry. I went to have a few words with the soldiers. The time is here is 12:37 a.m., my love.

Jenna: Okay, sweetheart. Go to sleep. You need your rest.

Eric: I wish I could hold you in my arms.

Jenna: I wish I was with you right now to give you that first kiss.

Eric: Oh, that would be nice.

Jenna: I can't wait to see you in person.

Eric: Honey, I promise you very soon, okay?

Jenna: Okay.

Eric: I will text you when I wake up.

Jenna: Okay, lover, see me in your dreams. XOXO.

Eric: Oh yes, I will kiss you in my dreams, my love.

Jenna: Feel me with you.

Eric: I love you so much, honey.

Jenna: I love you too. When I see you the first time, I am going to rock your world.

Eric: Oh, sweet, my love.

Jenna: I can't wait to hold your face and kiss you slowly and passionately.

April 7, 2018

Eric: Kisses and hugs to you, my love.
Eric: I love you so much. I will text you when I wake up.

* * * * *

I went to Hangouts today (October 7, 2019), and I can't find any of my feeds. None of the conversations that I had with Eric are in the feed. I am not sure if he had blocked me or if the application had blocked me, so I just have what else I wrote by hand.

I can fill in the blanks if I can get the application to show me the messages again; however, I may not be able to get the whole conversation on here now. I am not technologically savvy and can't figure out how the whole conversation was deleted. It had been on here for over a year, and now nothing.

* * * * *

April 17, 2018

Eric: I am on my short, honey, and yes, I have my own room.
Jenna: On your short?
Eric: Yes, my love.
Jenna: That is good you have your own room. I don't know what that
    means.
Eric: Hahaha, baby, you can see the size of my dick with what I am
    wearing right now.
Jenna: LOL. Does that mean you have underwear on or shorts, or are
    you naked and well-endowed? LOL.
Eric: Almost naked.
Jenna: Oh-la-la.
Eric: Hahahaha! Oh, you always have a way of making me laugh, my
    love.
Jenna: I wish I could be there. I would give you 100 percent. LMAO.
    Kidding.

Eric: LOL. But you own it, so there won't be any need for the money. All you have to do is say it. Baby, I need you, and I am all yours.

Jenna: So you are fifty-three, right? You are not a minor that I am talking to, I hope and pray.

Eric: I love it when my wife puts on crazy shorts when we are alone in the house. It drives me crazy. I am ready to go all the way, riding with her, baby.

Jenna: What are crazy shorts? I wear thongs. LOL.

Eric: Just pants. I love when my woman puts on only pants when we are alone in the house. It makes my head roll like dice in a casino game.

Jenna: So she would wear nothing on the top, just pants?

Eric: But only when we are alone in the house.

Jenna: LOL. I kind of got that.

Eric: What are you doing at the moment?

Jenna: Sitting in the car, texting. You should go to the gym.

Eric: Okay, honey. I will be sleeping before you get home. 'Night, my queen.

Jenna: Sleep well. Now I am going to be thinking of you naked. 😆 😆 😆 Oh yeah, some guy named David Brooks friended me. Is he an army guy of yours?

Eric: No, my love. I don't know him. You have to be careful. Most of the Taliban we are fighting against here are using our pictures to get through to our loved ones and track them down, okay? Please don't accept any military persons anymore because I don't want to lose you, honey, okay? Please block him.

Jenna: Okay.

Eric: My queen, you have to promise you are not going to accept any more request on FB.

Jenna: Okay.

Eric: I have a cousin that lives in California, and someone put her picture on my site and wanted to friend me. They didn't know anything about her family and wanted me to get into some kind of lottery. I asked who her husband was, and the person couldn't answer. I let Facebook know about it.

Eric: Now you know what I mean. Have you blocked the person?

Jenna: Yes, I did after I reported them to Facebook and after I told my cousin.

Eric: Good, baby.

Eric: Please be careful. I don't want to lose you.

Jenna: Tell me you are not one of those men, please. Please tell me you are the man in the picture. I am going to be sick if I am not helping a US soldier.

Eric: My queen, why would you say that to me? You have been saying that all the time. We have been together for a while now, and yet you don't trust me?

Jenna: Because you just put the idea in my head, and you have an accent. LOL. Sorry.

Eric: Why, my queen?

Jenna: I do trust you, but I need to ask, love. I need to be sure you are who you say you are.

Eric: My queen, I am the one in that picture you see. It is me. That is my picture you are seeing on my profile, honey.

Jenna: Okay, I hope that is your picture because this is the picture of the man that I am falling in love with. I haven't heard your voice, and I haven't seen your face. I just have your texts and your pictures, nothing else.

Eric: My queen, soon you are going to hear my voice, see me, and hold me tight in your arms.

Jenna: Okay, sweetheart. I hope that is you because no other man will do for me right now.

Eric: My queen, I told you to remove those negative thoughts from your mind, okay? I have to rest now. I love you so much.

Jenna: I can't wait to see the real, live man. Good night, my king. I am sorry I doubted you. I try to be positive, then my mind goes wild. I can't wait for the day that I am in your arms forever. I am sorry. I need to have faith that everything will work out as planned.

Jenna: I am in love with a man I have never met, his dog, his child, and his vision for the future. Please do not hurt my heart. You are what I live for. To you I give my complete devotion. I have never heard or seen you. How can this be that I have feelings for someone I have only been texting and have never touched? Your words, songs, and good-mornings have touched my heart. You have made me feel like I am the only one in your world and that you are happy with that. You want to marry me. How can that be? You have never seen me in person, only my pictures.

April 18, 2018

Eric: My queen, I dedicate my love and life to you. I promise never to hurt you, baby, no matter the challenges we both face in life. I swear to always stand by you forever. I thank God for everything, especially the first day I met you, honey. If I could wish for one thing right now, I'd wish we could see each other. I wish I could get out of here right now and embrace the future together. I promise you we are going to be with each other soon. I love you so much. Nothing is going to change that, honey. Good morning to you, my love. I hope you slept well.

Eric: Love has taken me to a new level where nothing counts except you and to a place where no one matters besides you. With you and just you alone, my life is made. You are of immeasurable value to me. I can't leave you for the world. I love you so much, my queen.

Eric: Honey, I am going on patrol right now. I will text you when am back, okay, my queen? I love you so much, my queen.

Jenna: I love you more. XOXO. Stay safe on patrol, for I cherish you as well. I am glad you have my back. Thank you. I can't wait to meet you.

Eric: Hello, my queen. I am back from patrol now, my love. I miss you so much, baby. Text me when you are free.

Jenna: Hi, love. I am here for you. They just had a party for me and cake and a card for the last day of my work.

Jenna: How was patrol, hon? Are you a doctor on patrol? Why a private hospital? I am curious. You must be asleep now. Know that I am thinking of you.

Eric: I am here now, my queen. No, I am not sleeping well, my love, and I can't sleep without telling my queen good night, baby.

My queen, I am not a doctor, and yes, it is going to be a private hospital. And we are going to have people working for us, okay, my love? We can't run the hospital alone. So we are gonna have nurses and doctors working for us, okay, my queen?

Jenna: Okay, love.

Eric: Honey, I am here now. I am sorry I nodded off, my queen.

Jenna: Hi, hon. My dad is in the hospital right now. I just got off the phone with my mom.

Eric: Oh my god, how is he doing?

Jenna: I just got off the phone with him. He seems good. He was talking to me. How was your day? I miss talking to you, or should I say texting you.

Eric: My love, he will be fine. I will pray for him.

Jenna: Thank you, love.

Eric: It is very late here, and yesterday was so stressful to me, baby.

Jenna: Oh no. Why was it stressful, love? I am sorry I am keeping you up.

Eric: Babe, it is still very early in the morning.

Eric: It is okay, my wife. I can't sleep without telling my queen good night.

Jenna: Oh, okay. Do you want to go back to sleep, love?

Eric: Babe, are you going to send the $70 to the company tomorrow?

Jenna: I will send them something. I am not sure how much I will be able to send.

* * * * *

I went back into my Hangouts, and all the conversations are gone. There's nothing left. It is like someone came in and erased everything that I and Eric wrote. Eric may not be his real name. It may be an alias. I did start writing down everything in a notebook; however, I have moved so much that I have lost notebooks along the way. I do have what I wrote in September, so I will write what I have now so that you know all the things that these people may say to you to get you to feel guilty and do what they want you to do.

September 1, 2018

Jenna: I am in love with the face with this man right here. [Jenna uploaded Eric's picture, the one that he gave me.] I love the way you look. I had a dream that when you came home to see me, instead of this man in the picture showing up, a teenage boy showed up. LOL. [This was her subconscious trying to tell her something.] The teenage boy said he took a picture of his father. I woke up after that.

*　*　*　*　*

In June I got my state license for insurance in New Hampshire, and I changed jobs after coding for sixteen and a half years.

*　*　*　*　*

Eric: LOL. You are so funny, babe. What are you doing at the moment, babe?
Jenna: I just took a shower. I'm ready to go to my first appointment.
Eric: Okay, babe. Look after yourself very well, dear.
Jenna: Okay, love. XOXO. You too. What is your day like? You must be in treatment? [Eric told Jenna he had been shot in the leg and was not able to go on patrol.

*　*　*　*　*

I think this may have been in August; however, I don't have that conversation in my Hangouts to check.

*　*　*　*　*

Jenna: I intuitively know that you are mine and that I am yours. There is no other man that I want to be with. [At this point, she had no idea that this chiseled, strong Caucasian face was not the man she was talking to.]

Jenna: when I look into your eyes, I see my soul and feel your presence in my heart. I feel you every day in my mind, and I am in love with you. However, sometimes my mind asks if this is really real, wondering if I will ever meet you or if this is a fantasy playing out.

September 2, 2018

Jenna: I hope you are okay. I hope nothing has happened to you. The site said you were active an hour ago. I hope this is correct? I am sending you my unconditional love. I hope you will feel this. [Jenna had not heard from Eric the whole day, which was not Eric's MO.]

Jenna: I am worried about you. If I did this to you, you wouldn't like it. I am worried, and I hope you are okay. [She thought that he was in a ditch somewhere, dead, or injured.]

September 3, 2018

Jenna: [She still received no answer from Eric.] I will be here for you whenever you come back. The Internet said you were active twenty-eight minutes ago. Sure, why can't you get in touch with me? Maybe you are keeping me silent. I know it is not the Internet because I have seen you online. Maybe you have found another queen. I know you told me before that you only talk to one woman at a time. I told you I have a lot of friends and talk to and a lot of people but that my heart is with one man, and that is you.

Jenna: To see you have been online but not hearing from you hurts. I will let you be. I won't bother you anymore. I am finally going to work on myself and try to get my life in order. Just know I love you and am thinking of you, and I will still hold the faith that you will speak to me soon. [By *speak to me*, Jenna meant "texting me"; she has never heard Eric's voice or seen Eric and did not know that the picture she had of Eric was not the real man that she was talking to.]

*   *   *   *

The silence from Eric was because my money went dry, so Eric had to find someone else to get money from at this time. I thought Eric was either hurt or dead from the war or that he found someone else to love. Yes, he found someone with a consistent supply money.

*   *   *   *

Jenna found out she had a West Palm Beach address on her credit report. She had never been to West Palm Beach.

September 3, 2018
5:51 p.m.

Eric: Hi, babe. How are you doing today? Where is my babe?
Jenna: What happened to you? I haven't heard from you since Saturday. If I did that to you, you would've been pissed with me.
Eric: The Internet was shut down. It goes on and off.
Jenna: So when it was on, why didn't you reach out?
Eric: Where are you at the moment?
Jenna: At home. Where are you?
Eric: I am here, babe. What have you been doing the whole day?
Jenna: What have you been doing the whole weekend?
Eric: Nothing, babe. You now I am not strong at the moment, nor do we have any good news yet.
Jenna: No, I have been applying online for loans for the past three hours. Before that, I walked six miles with my son. Before that, I listened to positive-thinking tapes. Everyone rescheduled because of the holiday.
Eric: Okay, babe. Have you gotten any loans yet?

Jenna: No, not yet, but it is a holiday. And on my credit report, there is a West Palm Beach address and a church street address that I have never lived in.

Eric: I guess that was a mistake, babe. Do you think we can get some luck tomorrow?

Jenna received a link from Eric with a caption that said, "It's fabulous I got my new boobies."

Jenna: If you were resting for two days, then who were you resting with?

Then Jenna sent the link that was sent to her through Eric's Hangouts account. Jenna was so worried that Eric found another woman. Jenna should have thought, *How did this woman buy her boobs? With whose money did she get them?*

Eric: BRB.

Jenna: Hmmm? I guess I can't say anything because I told you to go for it if you needed to. You also said I was the only one, but the last couple of weekends, you have disappeared, granted you had a great excuse for the last weekend, with your troops being shot. If this woman can afford big boobs, then she can afford to help you out of there. *BRB* was two hours ago, and you are still online. Do what is right for you, and I will do what is right for me. [Jenna had lost thousands of dollars from helping this man, and she didn't have any more money to send to Eric. Eric was getting bored talking to her because of that.]

Eric: What do you mean by that?

Jenna: No one likes to be ignored. If you are going on a date, then tell me. That way, I don't have to worry where you are for two days. You are in a war zone, and I worry about you. If you have possession of your phone and Internet, please just let me know somehow and some way that you are okay. That way, I will not worry about you. If you are going to be with someone, then okay. It will hurt but not as much as if you die.

Eric: If you really want me to be happy and stay alive, why not do what is necessary? Stop using words. Actions speak louder than words. You have been saying you are trying, but there is no good news yet [meaning, no more money for Eric].

Jenna: I have had six weeks without a paycheck. Do you think I want that? I am not doing this to hurt you. I am trying every day, going into people's homes and showing the plans. A lot of people are worse off than I am. At least I have a roof over my head and food on the table.

Jenna: You have no idea what I am going through to help you. I am reaching out to different places to see about making more money.

Jenna: When I had money to give you, I gave it to you every single time. Don't you ever say I am not doing everything in my power to get you out of there! Just because you can't see the money doesn't mean I am sitting on my ass, doing nothing! I have been busy, and I still check on you.

September 5, 2018

Eric: Hi, babe. How are you doing today? [Seriously, I ripped him a new one, and all he had was "Hi, babe. How are you doing today?" How did he think she was doing?]

Jenna: Good. I had a small sale yesterday, and I am presenting tonight. How are you doing?

Eric: Sad.

Jenna: Why? Please talk to me.

Eric: Things are not good over here.

Jenna: Oh no! what is wrong?

Eric: I told you I need to get out of here. Up till now, I have no money.

Jenna: I know. I am sorry for that. Things are looking up now, love.

* * * * *

At this point, I should have blocked his ass. Now, reading and writing this again makes me so upset as to how gullible I was.

*   *   *   *   *

Eric: No solution.

Jenna: I miss the Eric I used to know.

Eric: I miss the Jenna I used to know.

Eric: The Jenna that is full of surprises [meaning, the Jenna who had money to give him].

Jenna: You mean the Jenna that used to get paid every other week, that had a consistent paycheck, and that sent money to you each and every time she got paid? I gave to you freely without paying any of my bills. I want a paycheck too. I don't get the money I used to get. I have a feeling that when I finally come up with your $3,200, you will have something else that needs to be paid right away. It seems as though when my money dried up, so did your love for me.

Jenna: I could say that I am in a financial bind because of your box. I would never say that, though, because I freely gave you what I had with gratitude for the love I had found with you. You gave me the sweetest love I have ever experienced, and now that I don't have money to give you, your love has left. And all I can feel from you is resentment!

Jenna: Why don't you look at what I have done for you already? Has anyone ever drained their bank account for you? Your statement surprises me, and it makes me sad that you are seeing me in a different light because I don't have the funds right now to give you.

Jenna: This in this song is what I thought we had. [The song was "As Far as I Can See."] Was I mistaken? Did I mean anything to you?

Eric: I told you $3,200 is all. Why do you think we will make another payment?

Jenna asked Eric to look at his email. Jenna thought someone had her password and wanted to tell Eric outside Hangouts.]

Eric: Why would you want us to email? Nobody has your password. We can talk on Hangouts.

Eric: The last payment was for my box, and up till now, we have not done anything about it. The company is not happy with us. The only solution is if you come up with that amount so that I can leave here, yet you are not doing anything about it. ☹☹☹

Eric: I told you everything that's going on. You can contact the company yourself.

Eric: Http://courier.crudexpress.com. You said nothing about it. Have a nice day.

Jenna: You too. There was nothing to tell. I've had no check for six weeks. I didn't want to be redundant.

Eric: I told you the job is not paying. Come to think of it, if the job is not paying, maybe you should have left them a long time ago. But you didn't. Wow.

Jenna: I am not going to get into a debate about it. I am not going to leave until I find another job just in case it picks up. I have the potential to make $2,500 a week with this job down the line.

Jenna: If you don't like it, maybe you should find yourself a sugar mama. I don't want to feel any worse than I already do. I feel like a failure, and the way you are talking to me doesn't help!

Jenna: One thing I have noticed is that when I have money to give you, I am your queen and your wife, but when I don't, I become your babe. Wow. I wouldn't ever make you feel that way. What Have you done for yourself lately? I had money to get out of this place that I am in. I had money to put down on my car payments. Now that I have helped you with your box, I am having a hard time paying my credit cards. Instead I put all of my money into your box. Now that I am having a hard time, it feels like you are looking down on me. I am destitute because I saw a man that I truly admire and love and a man that I wanted to give all I had to make happy. I want you out of the war zone, but unfortunately, my hands are tied right now.

Jenna: Do what you want. I am tired and emotionally drained. I love you unconditionally, and I want to be with you. However, I have been alone, by myself, as well, and I also like that. As much as I admire and love you, I can also live alone very well once I start making money.

Eric: Wow, you said I am looking down on you? Thank you for the rude words. It does not matter. Always know that I care about you and love you so much. Like I said before, and I will still say it again, your money will be paid back when I leave here.

* * * * *

It is almost 2020 when I am typing all this out, and I have not seen one cent of the money he promised to pay.

* * * * *

Eric: Good morning. Have a blessful day.

Jenna: I have no doubt you will pay me back. [Eric had no intention of paying her back.] I just don't like the way you have been treating me lately. You have changed because I don't have money. [Jenna was bringing lack to herself, telling him that she did not have money.] I am trying to stay positive, and I am working around the clock. But it hasn't come to fruition yet. Every time I let you down, I feel bad. I am being honest with you and letting you know how it feels. It takes time to learn a whole new industry. Each time I bring up my failures, I bring that same experience back into my life.

Jenna: I need to have faith that God has a plan for all of us. There is a reason that this is not falling into place for us right now. I trust God and the universe to lead me to the correct path. I do love you, and I always will. [Jenna had since realized that this would not be the case because the man she loved didn't exist.]

Jenna: I know I probably won't hear from you this weekend. It has been that way for a few weeks now. I know you are not allowed to tell me why, but the way it looks to me is that you have found someone else. Am I correct in my thinking? Or is it something you don't want to tell me or talk about? Either way, if I am your woman, I have to tell you this. Women do not like to be ignored, and no woman likes to be ghosted. Have a blessed weekend.

Sept 8, 2018

Eric: I have no other woman, okay? You are the only one I have, and you know that. How will I be happy when things are not going as planned? How will I be happy when I almost died a few days back?

Jenna: Well, you never told me that, and I am not a mind reader, although I would like to be. I was going to say that you and I have a six-month anniversary tomorrow. I don't know what to do. I feel that my hands are tied behind my back and I can't get out of the grip.

Jenna: What happened to you, and are you all right now?

Eric: I am okay now. Where are you at the moment?

Jenna: I just had a presentation but no sale. The girl can't afford it.

Eric: Okay. That is nice. Can Jerry [his son] get $100 from you please?

Jenna: I would if I could. I don't have $100 to give.

Eric: Okay, hon. Before you send it, let me know first.

Jenna: Okay.

Eric: Where are you at the moment?

Jenna: I'm in Manchester. I'm going to meet another agent at a client's. Where are you?

Eric: I am in the camp. I will go for medical treatment soon.

Jenna: Thank you for letting me know, love. I pray that you will be great. I pray that you will be healthy, but if not, I want to heal you back to health.

Eric: Thank you, sweetie. I hope you are doing okay.

Jenna sent Eric "The Wind Beneath My Wings."

Jenna: I am doing well. I went with Carmen to an apartment. Now I have to drive her back to get some dinner. I miss you. I am doing okay. I would be doing better if I made some money.

Eric: God is in control.

Jenna: Yes, God is.

Eric: Good morning, babe. How was your night? And how are you doing?

Jenna: Good morning, my king. Happy anniversary. My night was good. I went over to Caitlin's and met her boyfriend. They make a cute couple. How was your day? Did you sleep well? How was your treatment? I am trying to get a hold of Ginger. High tide is at 11:00 a.m. today and on Tuesday. I'm not sure when Sue wants to go. We need to go at low tide, not high tide. I have to wait until she gets back to me.

Eric: Okay. What are you doing at the moment?

Jenna: What do you mean, babe?

Eric: That we have to do it next week isn't working.

Jenna: It is going to rain on Tuesday, and I can't take pictures in the rain.

Jenna: You are the fresh, new beginning. Yes, I did have someone that was a narcissist, and I divorced him. I am focusing on getting money in, and I guess I have been pushing aside love but not all the way. But I do love you. [Jenna loved the thought of being in love and loved the picture that this scammer sent to her.] I want the money to get to you and also money to keep my car. Yes, I am struggling financially. I don't want to throw this relationship away. I love you very much.

Eric: Same here, my love. I love you so much, and it hurts me that things are like this.

Jenna: Me too. I am not sure how to change this to make money. We need to make this right. I think I need to get away from this job, which is not working for me. I don't have another job lined up. I was sleeping when you wrote that.

Jenna: Today I need to figure out how to help you get out of here. Are you here with me, my love?

Eric: I am here, babe. What did you figure out, babe?

Jenna: My part-time job from Dr. K. He is coming back from his vacation, so I can work from there when he gets back. I went to a woman named Gabrielle to see about setting up my Reiki table. I am working on my photography, and my friend Ginger

had me sing for her singer friend from Nashville. He said I have
a great voice.

Jenna: I don't know what will take off in flight, but something has to
come to fruition. I know this job is not working for me, but I
need to stick with it until I find something else.

Eric: I understand you, babe. We have to act fast. What are your
plans today?

Jenna: I have to go in and make phone calls today. I am going to
some hotels to see if they are hiring. I really don't want to be in
this house anymore.

Eric: Thank God and you, babe, for the idea. When you are less busy,
let me know, okay?

Jenna had her earbuds on her phone, and her phone started
typing by itself without her seeing it because the earbuds were on her
screen. This is what it typed. The first word that was typed was *fog*,
then a lot of *x*s and sevens and also whole words. And then there were
bunches of *ixxi*s and *xxi*s for six lines. And then on the seventh line
were actual letters. It was like the angels were talking to her through
*xxi*s, telling her to get out of her situation. Jenna didn't want to be
there anymore. Then there were bunches of *I*s and bunches of *c*s and
*x*s before Jenna saw what her phone had sent.

Jenna: LOL. My earbuds typed this while I was in the shower. The
wire was lying on my keyboard of my phone.

Jenna: I started typing you a message, I put my earbuds down to get
into the shower, and it actually wrote the words by itself.

Jenna: I am sorry, babe, for being busy. I love you with all my heart.

Eric: Same here, babe.

Jenna: Going into work now.

Eric: Okay.

September 10, 2018

Jenna: I need to get a full-time job and do it. This part-time is not
working out for me. I talked to my boss. They think I am too

nice to work in this business. They think I should do something with health insurance.

Eric: Good. Remember, I told you all this, and you were thinking I didn't want the best for you.

Jenna: I know you want the best for me [he really didn't want the best for Jenna] and I want to make some money to get the heck out of here.

Eric: I know, babe.

Jenna: If not this, then something better.

Eric: Have you eaten, babe? [They always ask this question and "Where are you?"]

Eric: Babe, when are you going to send the $100 to our son? [Eric said *our son* to make Jenna believe that they would be a family. Just know that she had never laid eyes on this man or married him and did not have a son with him.]

Jenna: I won't have money until next week. Please tell him I am sorry. [Jenna held a lot of guilt and stress. She had been in the field every single day and night and had not had luck in selling life insurance.]

Eric: Hmmm?

Jenna: Remember, today rained, and tomorrow is going to bring thunderstorms. I can't take pictures outside, in the rain.

Jenna: Thank you for being there for me today. I am sorry I couldn't send any money to Jerry. I haven't received a check yet.

Eric: I am here, babe.

Jenna: Hi, love. I wish I woke up in time. XO. I miss you.

Eric: I miss you too, babe.

Jenna: How has your day been? I am working the flea market with my ex-BF / roommate now, Darren. I should make a little money but not much. I'm working here so I can help pay for rent. I don't like to take much from him.

September 11, 2018

Jenna: You must be asleep. Sweet dreams, my love.

Eric: Good morning, babe. How are you doing today?

Jenna: Good morning, love.

Eric: How was your night, babe?

Jenna: It was okay. How was yours? I am about to do this meditation called Change Your Life in 7 Days. I am preparing myself for greatness, and abundance is coming into my life.

Eric: Were you able to go out and search for a job?

Jenna: The Internet. It is 8:30 a.m., and I have an 11:00 a.m. appointment. Then I have an AAPC meeting tonight. In between I will look, love.

Jenna: The client was not home, UGH! So I am applying for Lyft job. It's $35 an hour, driving people around in my car, in Manchester.

Eric: Okay. Please look after yourself very well. I hope you are okay, babe.

Jenna: Yes. I had an AAPC meeting. How was your day today?

Eric: Good morning, my beautiful babe.

Jenna: How are you doing? What are your plans for today?

Jenna: I am feeling a little sad, but I am okay.

Eric: What is wrong, babe?

Jenna: I have come to the conclusion that I have to let my insurance job go. It is not working for me. I feel like I failed, and I am usually not like that. I am feeling defeated, and I need to stop this altogether and get another job.

Eric: What are your plans for now?

Jenna: I need to go into work and let them know, then I will take the Marriott online full-time and do Lyft part-time.

Eric: Okay. Remember, I brought this idea up, and you thought it was not right.

Jenna: We have new officers that are coming in this year. It was announced at our last meeting. So I will be stepping down as president this year, after December. Right now I am closing many doors and praying for something better. When one door closes somewhere, another window will also open.

Jenna: Yes, you could see it. I guess I didn't want to see it because I worked so hard to get it. I can't go on like I have been anymore. I have become this person I don't even know. I wanted to lose all the weight I gained, and I have lost weight because of not having money to buy food. So I guess this job made me lose weight, which I had asked God to help me do.

Jenna: I am praying to God to guide me to the correct path or job so I can pay for my phone and car.

Eric: 😢😢😢

Jenna: I never asked how you are doing.

Eric: How are you doing, and what are you doing at the moment? I thank God for life.

Jenna: I thank God for keeping you safe.

Eric: Where are you at the moment?

Jenna: I'm at the house, working on applications.

Eric: Okay. Have you eaten?

Jenna: Are you back at your barracks, or do you have to go on road duty? I haven't eaten much. How about you? My wish is that you are totally healthy and happy. My love for you is everlasting and strong. I love you. God, please protect Eric wherever he may be.

Eric: Hi, babe. How are you doing?

Jenna: Hi. I am doing better and updated my resume.

Eric: Okay, babe. I hope you are doing very well.

Jenna: Yes. I shared an English muffin with Milo, the dog. I am trying to apply for the Marriott front-desk position. I hope you are doing well. Hey, why have I turned into babe again instead of your wife or your queen? LOL.

Eric: LOL. You own all the sweetest names in this world.

Jenna: LOL. Great answer. You get big points for that one, my love.

September 15, 2018

Eric: How are you doing?

Jenna: How are you?

Eric: I'm not feeling okay.

Jenna: What is going on?

Eric: Yesterday was a hectic day.

Jenna: What happened? I am worried about you today. It is not a good day for the flea market. It's overcast and drizzling. It was supposed to be eighty degrees.

Eric sent me a picture of a rose with pearls.

Jenna: Awww, thank you, my love.
Eric: What have you been doing the whole time today?
Jenna: Selling at the flea market. I have a little money to send to Jerry, not a lot. Every little bit helps.
Eric: How much, babe? Can you please talk to me?
Jenna: It's $42, and $8 has to be for the fee.
Eric: Okay, babe. Let me forward the details for you. Hold on. You are going to send this to an Alex in Ghana. Have you seen it, babe?
Jenna: Is Alex a girl or a guy?
Eric: No, Alex is a grown man.
Jenna: Why am I not sending the money to Whitney, Jerry's teacher?
Eric: What time are you going to send it?
Jenna: I am heading there now.
Eric: Okay, honey. Thanks a lot.
Jenna: Is it Alex or Alexander? This is just in case they ask me.
Eric: Babe, please make sure you spell it well.
Jenna: Yes, so it was $46 altogether.
Eric: I got it, babe. Thank you so much. I am going to forward it to him right now.

Jenna had taken a picture of the receipt for him to send to the new person, Alex. Eric still did not explain why another person was all of a sudden getting this money.]

Jenna: Okay.
Eric: Are you going home now?
Jenna: No, I am working part-time, selling insurance, while I look for another job.
Eric: Okay, babe. Look after yourself very well, babe.

Jenna: I always do. I know kickboxing, if anyone tries to mess with
me. I would put up a fight and check under my fingernails
because their DNA will be there.
Eric: Hahahahahah! 😂 🥺
Eric: Babe, how are you doing? Good morning, my beautiful wife.
[Now that Jenna had sent some money to him, she was his
beautiful wife again even though they were never ever married.]
Jenna: Good morning, my handsome husband. I just did a medi-
tation and am getting ready to take pictures at the beach with
Gabrielle.

Jenna had Gabrielle take a picture of her so she could send it
to Eric.

Jenna: Why are you so quiet today?
Eric: Babe, am not quiet, okay? I just saw your message. How are
you doing?
Jenna: I am doing well. How are you doing?
Eric: How was your flea market today? I hope it went well.
Eric: Wow, babe, you look beautiful.
Jenna: Awww.
Eric: Okay. I hope it is safe for you, babe.

I sent pictures of the beach to Eric.

Eric: Beautiful, babe. How is my babe doing?

September 17, 2018
1:55 a.m.

Jenna: Your babe was sleeping. How was your day? It was a long day
yesterday.
Eric: My day was okay, honey. Jerry sends his greetings, babe. Thank
you for the money. It will go a long way for them.
Jenna: Good, I am glad I could finally help. How is Jerry doing?
Eric: He is better than he was before.

Jenna: What happened? Are you talking about when he was in the hospital?

Eric: No, he is not, honey. You know it has been long since we sent him money, honey, and things were not in the right place. But the money you sent will go a long way for them. How are you doing?

Jenna: I am doing okay but a little tired.

Eric: You need to get some rest, babe.

Jenna: I am glad Jerry is getting better. So is Whitney not with Jerry? I am okay. I just woke up. I got in at 12:00 p.m. I downloaded pictures at Gabrielle's and cropped them.

September 17, 2018
6:22 p.m.

Jenna: Who are you? What are you all about? Are you for real? For six months, we have texted, and we have never heard each other's voices? We have laughed, cried, and fought. We have bonded with each other, but how did this come to be? Are you the man in this picture, or are you a person I have made up in my mind? Are you the person that is in the picture, or are you someone totally different? All are questions that I have with no apparent answers. I know I haven't made you up because I see a text from you almost every day.

Jenna: The only explanation is that you are someone I knew before in a different life. Or are you my destiny in this life? When I look into your eyes, I see my reflection in you. I pray that you are the man in the picture that you sent me. I pray that you are my other half. You are a mystery that I want solved. I want answers, but for whatever reason, you are not able to give me the answer yet. I have faith that in time, the answers will come. If not this, then there's something better. I love your smile, the dimple on your cheek when you smile, and your chiseled cheekbones. I pray that in time, you will let me know about you and what makes you tick.

The Mystery Man

Eric: You are my everything, babe. You know I remain Eric, my babe and my everything.

Jenna: Awww, you are my everything, and I can't wait to finally meet you.

Eric: What are you doing, babe? Babe, are you with me?

Jenna was taking a shower, and her earbuds were on her phone screen. On September 17, at 9:29 a.m., her phone typed a message to her while she was in the shower. There were bunches of letters and numbers, mostly *x*s and sevens. And words also came up. Jenna thought it was her angels trying to get a message to her. Here are the words that that were spelled out: *Kim, jealous, milk, immunization, out, kook, immobility, Molokai,* and *multimillion. U171* came out a couple of times, and there were a lot of *Ki*s, *M*s, *UKK*s, and sevens.

Jenna: My earbuds were with you while I was in the shower and were still writing when I got out to wipe off.

Jenna: Talk about a mystery. What are the angels trying to tell us?

Eric: LOL. What are your plans today?

Jenna: I am going to work. I have three appointments tomorrow.

Eric: Okay, babe. Please look after yourself.

Jenna: I met a woman last night who is a manager for a health insurance company, and she is getting me into her office for an interview.

Eric: Wow, that is nice. So she is going to secure a job for you?

Jenna: Yes, she is.

Jenna: In my twenties, I read the Bible all the way through twice, the King James Version.

Jenna: So I looked at the message again that our angels sent, and "Molokai is a Hawaiian island in Central Pacific on the islands northern Kalaupapa Peninsula. It is a steep path leading to Kalaupapa National Historic Park, an isolated former leper colony below tower cliffs. The site can be viewed by the cliff top nearby the path phallic rock. It is said to have fertility powers. About 260 miles, population 7404 in 2000."

Jenna: Hey, maybe you should build your private hospital in Molokai.

Eric: That is just the plan, honey. Remember, I told you that before, and we have come to the conclusion of building it. But things are not going very well.

Jenna: No? Why, love? Is it because of your box?

Eric: Yes, babe. 😠😠😠😟😟😟

Jenna: I know. I wish I could help more.

Eric: I need to get out of here and fix things.

Jenna: Yes, I am trying to work on that.

Eric: I know you don't have more, and it hurts me because I should be the one taking care of you and paying all your bills.

Jenna: Don't worry about that right now. Let's concentrate on getting you out of the situation you can get hurt in. Then go and get your son, and then you can get your money. We will all figure this out together.

Jenna: I hope you realize I love you for you and not for your fortune, which you may or may not have. If you are able to acquire your box, I will be so happy for you because I know how much it means to you and how it will make you happy. If you don't get it back, I still want to be with you through good times or bad.

Eric: Honey, when I am out of here, I will come over to meet you first before sending for Jerry. After leaving here, I will have access to money, okay? I have a lot to offer you, and I promise not to let you down.

Jenna: You haven't let me down yet. I will be so happy to see you here with me.

Eric: God will always protect you before I get home, okay? I love you always, babe.

Jenna: May God protect you and keep you safe. I can't wait to help you and build your dream. I love you more, my love.

Eric: Babe, you are the queen of my kingdom. Without my queen, I have no kingdom.

Jenna: Without my king, I would be lost.

Eric: We are going to do it together, babe.

Jenna: Yes, I believe that will happen.

Eric: You are the most beautiful girl that ever happened to come into
    my life.
Jenna: you are the most precious man. You are my rock, solid, sturdy,
    and will protect me throughout life's storms. You are my most
    precious stone.
Jenna: Eric, the message from the angels is significant. I believe there
    is a higher power working for us behind the scenes. God has a
    plan in mind, and I trust that he has our best interests at heart.
Eric: You rule my world, babe.
Jenna: I feel the same about you. I look forward to the day we can be
    together and the day we can actually talk to each other. I want
    to wrap my arms around you and kiss you too.
Eric: I love you always.
Jenna: I love you more. What is the meaning of *Quansah*? What is
    your nationality?
Eric: "Ever" or "eternal." My nationality is American.
Jenna: I love that it fits you well. I want to know you inside and out.
    I am falling for my king head over heels again.

September 17, 2018

Eric: Smile. You are the best, babe.
Jenna: I love you.
Eric: I love you always. What are you doing at the moment?
Jenna: I made a sale. It doesn't come until Thursday.
Eric: Okay, babe. Good sale? Will it be enough?
Jenna: I'm not sure, babe, but I think I did good. People are high-fiv-
    ing me.
Eric: Okay. Do you know how much it is?
Jenna: I'm not sure, babe, but I have another appointment tomorrow.
Eric: Okay, my love. Honey, it's late already, and you need to eat,
    okay?
Jenna: I will eat when I get home. I love you. You made a difference
    in my day today. I am so glad I met you.
Jenna: Thank you, my love, for a wonderful day today. I pray yours
    was as good.

Eric: Sweet dreams, babe. I love you always.

Jenna: I love you too.

Eric: Good morning, babe.

Jenna: Good morning, love. I wish I was making you breakfast in bed.

Eric: Thank you for that, babe. I prefer to wake you up with kisses and tender love.

Jenna: Mmmm, that would be the first thing we would do, and breakfast the second thing.

Jenna: I have an interview at 9:30 a.m. today, and I have a 6:00 p.m. appointment tonight. I want to go into the office and book up, and I would like to stay connected with you, love.

Eric: Okay, love. Have you taken your shower?

Jenna: Yes, I have now. I am going out to the interview, and it is very wet outside. We are getting the hurricane down south.

Eric: Okay. Please be careful, babe.

Jenna: I will. I just got to the office now.

Eric: Okay, babe. How did it go?

Jenna: Good. I have a second interview tomorrow.

Eric: Okay, babe. I miss you, my love.

Jenna: I miss you too. How is your day going?

Eric: My day is okay, babe. And yours?

Jenna: It is good. The rain has stopped, yeah.

Eric: Okay. Are you still there, babe?

Jenna: I came to the house. I had to get on my computer to do a module, then I'm going to a client's house.

Jenna: UGH! They weren't home.

Eric: I miss you, babe.

Sept 19, 2018

Jenna: I miss you too. I am going into my second interview now.

Eric: I wish you good luck, my beautiful wife. 😙 😙 😙

Jenna: I got the position.

Eric: Good news, babe! We are going to celebrate this.

Jenna: Yes, we are, babe. XOXO.

Jenna: Now I told my current job, and they are happy for me.

Eric: When will you start?

Jenna: They want me to train. I am helping someone book appointments at my job now.

Eric: I am asking if you are going to be starting your new job and asking how much they are going to be paying you.

Jenna: Open enrollment starts on October 15 for Medicare, and November 1 is for individual insurance. Probably next week? I have already started to train.

Eric: Oka, but did you find out the payment?

Jenna: Oh, for the sale I had? No, not yet.

Eric: For the new job, how much will they be paying you? And how many hours will you be working?

Jenna: I don't know how it works. They pay on commission and said they pay in advance. And when open enrollment comes, I maybe will be working a lot. For now I want to make as much as I can.

Eric: Okay, babe. When is the enrollment?

Jenna: It's October 15 for Medicare and November 1 for under-sixty-five insurance.

Eric: Okay, honey, but this is going to take a long time.

Jenna: This is a blessing for me from the universe. They advance your pay. I believe it will be better, I hope.

Eric: It's good to hear that.

Jenna: Yes, love, it will be better then.

Eric: I will pray over it.

Jenna: Yes, babe.

Jenna: Your prayers will be answered. Will you really be coming for me after, when you are out? So I looked at the clock, and it says 7:17 p.m., your birthday. I miss you.

Eric: Babe, I will come for you. You know I will.

Eric: I may not be with you this morning, but I am sending you my love so that you can wake up and have a good morning.

Jenna: Awww, you are the best man ever.

Eric: Same here, babe. How are you doing, babe? I miss you.

Jenna: I miss you too. I'm going into the insurance company. I am leaving. I got off the phone with the creditors.
Eric: Okay, babe. I trust you.
Eric: Okay, honey. Do you have any good news yet?
Jenna: No, I won't see it until tomorrow. How are you, sweetheart?
Eric: Okay, babe. Are you going to try and send some money tomorrow, babe?
Jenna: I need to look and see how much I get, babe.
Eric: Okay, babe. I trust you. Thank you for everything.
Jenna: I was in a meeting.

September 20, 2018

Eric: How are you doing, my wife? I guess you are busy.
Jenna: My job just sent me home. I can't be working for HealthMarkets and them at the same time because of conflict of interest.
Eric: What are you going to do about this now, hon?
Jenna: I am going with the other job. I believe it is the better job. It will be busier. If it doesn't work out, I will go into retail again.
Eric: Good, the idea you brought is okay. Where are you at the moment?
Jenna: I am going to my friend Bonnie's in Concord. I don't want to be at the house.
Eric: Okay, hon.
Jenna: I am used to giving two weeks' notice not being went home? Now I am not sure when I will get my last check.
Eric: But you said you will know on Thursday, which is today.
Jenna: No, on Friday. Today is Thursday, love.
Eric: Okay, babe. Have you seen Bonnie?
Jenna: Yes, she is a good friend. I am at Dunkin' Donuts right now, waiting for her to get out of work. I haven't seen her yet but will be going there soon.
Eric: Okay, babe. Please be careful, okay?
Jenna: I will let you know when I get home.
Eric: Okay, babe. Kisses.
Jenna: Kisses and hugs. I am at the house now.

Eric: You just came back, honey?

Jenna: Yes, it is about forty-five minutes away from my home. Bonnie has pie and coffee, love.

Eric: Okay, hon. What are your plans for tomorrow, babe?

Jenna: I have to get my check and cash it. I have to go to Salem to pay for a background check and pay some on my care and for an oil change.

Eric: Honey, you should have sent first before any other thing.

Jenna: Sent what first, love?

Eric: Sent the money first.

Jenna: Yes, I will send it when I go and cash my check.

Eric: Okay, that is a good idea. I miss you. I was here, waiting for you.

Jenna: Awww, I was thinking of you too. Thank you for waiting for me.

Eric: You are highly welcome.

Jenna: You are the only man that fills my heart with love.

Eric: Without you, I am empty, babe.

Jenna: Mmmm, without you I would be lost.

Jenna sent Eric the man's picture that Eric sent to her.

Jenna: This is the man that I can't wait to meet.

Eric: Soon, babe. Our dreams are working out for us.

Jenna: Yes, they are. I hope you are not disappointed in the way I look. I don't look like my picture with Sydney, my dog now. That was ten years ago. My body is good for my age, but it is not as muscular as yours.

Eric: Both of us are younger for each other, okay?

Jenna: Okay, baby. I love you.

Eric: I love you, babe. I need to get some rest now. I have a lot to do later.

Jenna: I love you too. I was just going to say that, love, okay? I am sorry for keeping you up. Go get some rest for me, and I will meet you in my dreams.

Eric: Okay, babe. Kisses and hugs. Love you always, babe.

Jenna: I love you too. Kisses and hugs. And feel me lying beside you, kissing you, and nuzzling into your neck.

September 21, 2018
5:28 a.m.

Eric: The light that shines from you is more vital to me than the light from the morning sun. Rise and shine, my beautiful queen. Good morning.

Jenna: Good morning to my king. I heard you in my dreams. I just woke up and feel the same for you.

Eric: Good. How is my babe this morning?

Jenna: I am tired but good. How are you doing?

Eric: Same here. What time is it over there?

Jenna: It is 5:46 a.m.

Eric: It is 2:23 p.m. here.

Jenna: Ahh, are you in your home or still at work?

Eric: I am still at work.

Jenna: How is your leg? It is healed?

Eric: Yes, it is healed, but I still feel pain inside.

Jenna: I will work on the pain for you, my love. I will use Reiki to make the pain move out of your leg.

Eric: Thank you, babe. I can't wait to feel your lovely arms.

Jenna: I can't wait to look into your stunning eyes and hold your handsome face in my hands.

Eric: I love you always, babe. What time are you going out this morning?

Jenna: I love you more. The office doesn't open until 9:30 a.m., and the checks don't come in until after 10:00 a.m.

Eric: Oh, okay, babe. So before 11:00 a.m., everything will be done.

Jenna: I will pray on it, baby. I need to get to the office, then get to Walmart, get through the line, etc. I will let you know when I have it, love.

Eric: Okay, babe. Do you have the details already?

Jenna: You are the light on this dismal day.

Eric: Kisses, babe.

Jenna: Your babe was in Walmart. My check does not amount to very much. I did pay on my Capital One card, so you should be able to use that once the payment goes through. I also have to pay for the background check and credit report as well.

Eric: How much are you sending?

Eric: Babe, leave that for now. You have to leave that for now. You have to send money first. We both agreed on this a few days ago. Why did you change your mind about this?

Jenna: Stop. I am trying to figure out how much I can send you. Please be patient.

Eric: Okay. Are you still in Walmart, babe?

Jenna: I'm in the parking lot.

Eric: Okay. What are your plans now?

Jenna: I need to pay for the background check, then I can send you $70. I am sorry I can't send more, but we can use the Capital One card as well once the payment goes through. Even though I made a great sale, my check was really small. I am trying to get my credit score up so I can get a loan.

Eric: Okay. Can you send it now and make it $100, honey?

Jenna: The line is out the door.

Eric: So when are you going to do it? Babe, here are the details again. The name Alex I. in Ghana.

Jenna: Okay.

Eric: Are you still busy, babe?

Jenna: Yes, baby. I'm taking a test at the new job. Walmart is right up the street. I had an appointment with my manager.

Eric: Okay. When are you going to be done, before going to Walmart?

Jenna: I am done. I am going to pay. I don't have $100. I only have $70. Who is this Alex? This is on the up and up, right? Why am I sending this to Alex? Whitney is Jerry's teacher.

Eric: Yes, send it to Alex. He is with Jerry. Go and send it now. Whitney is not around. That is why you are sending it to Alex.

Jenna: Okay. What is the telephone number?

Eric: Why, babe? What is going on?

Jenna: I am in Walmart, a big store, and you have to fill out a form even though the person is in the system.

Eric: Okay.

Jenna: Which province of Ghana is Alex in?

Eric: Accra is the state.

Jenna: What is the province?

Eric: Why do you have so many questions? The country is Ghana, and the state Accra.

Jenna: LOL. It's too simple. Do you want money? Do you want a MoneyGram or Walmart2World?

Eric: MoneyGram.

Jenna: Ugh, now there is a huge line.

Eric: Honey, how about where you have been sending from? Is it the same Walmart?

Jenna: Yes. I am going back there.

Eric: Are you going there now?

Jenna: No, I'm in traffic now.

Eric: Okay. When are you going to do it, babe?

Jenna: I sent the receipt. Did you get it?

Eric: Hi, babe. I was sleeping. Thank you so much, babe.

Jenna: Hi, baby.

Eric: I love you.

Jenna: Oh, I am sorry for waking you. Please go back to sleep.

Eric: Thank you, babe. I love you always.

Jenna: I love you too. There's no need to thank me. You can do that when you get here. I will meet you in my dreams.

Eric: Good morning, beautiful. You are the most generous, loving person that I know, and I am so blessed to have you in my life. Have a truly amazing day, my love.

Jenna: Good morning to my king, or is this your afternoon? I am taking pictures for a fiftieth anniversary for my friend's mother and father in Haverhill, Massachusetts.

Jenna: I just did a hypnosis session for attracting money.

Eric: Hi, babe.

Jenna: Hi.

Eric: How are you doing?

Jenna: Good. I'm on my way to Winnekenni Castle in Haverhill, Massachusetts, to take pictures.

Eric: Okay, babe.

Jenna: I got home. You must be asleep. I hope you are the real Eric. I pray that you are thinking of me. I hope you are not some past creep that hates me for leaving him and wants me to pay and believe he is someone else. 😆 😆 😆

Eric: Sweet dreams, my love. I will meet you in my dreams, love. I love you with all my heart.

Eric: Hi, love. How are you doing?

Jenna: Hi, my king. I am doing okay. I feel like I am getting a cold. I just took some cough medicine, some allergy medicine, and vitamin C with rosehip. Hopefully, it will go away. How are you doing?

Eric: That's sad. I will get back to you.

Jenna: It is okay. I will be okay. I would love to sleep in your arms and cuddle up close to you. You must be busy. It is 4:36 a.m. here. I may fall back asleep, hon. I will be with you in my dreams. You will get back to me? What does that mean, love? I hope you are okay.

Eric: I'm not okay. I'm trying to fix something. Jerry needs to renew his traveling documents in Ghana.

Jenna: Oh no.

Eric: My son is in danger. Whitney is not around.

Jenna: What is going on?

Eric: Getting all the papers renewed is going to cost $2,800.

Jenna: Oh God, please help Jerry wherever he is. Please protect him and keep him safe.

September 23, 2018
1:39 p.m.

Jenna: Know that I am here for you when you need me. I am giving you space to work out the situation with Jerry. I am keeping both of you in my thoughts and prayers and in light and love.

September 24, 2018
5:22 a.m.

Eric: Hi, honey. They said to contact the MoneyGram service to complete transaction. They cannot pick it up. Was the money not sent? MoneyGram did not complete the transaction.

Eric: Did you get the message I sent you?

Jenna: I got the message. Sorry I fell asleep. I don't know why it didn't send.

Eric: I don't know also.

Jenna: I am starting my new job today. I don't have more money to send.

Eric: Listen, I am talking about the $70 you sent. They could not pick it up. You have to go back there and find out why they cannot pick it up. Do you get me now? I am talking about this receipt.

Jenna: Walmart is not open. It is 5:00 a.m.

Eric: Okay, honey. Once they open, find out, okay? If they don't give a better reason, take the money and go to Western Union, okay?

Jenna: I don't know why it didn't send. I will have to call?

Eric: What time does Walmart open?

Jenna: I think 8:00 a.m.

Eric: How will you be able to do it, honey?

Jenna: I don't know. I don't know why it didn't send. I am not sure I will have time to send it through Western Union.

Eric: Honey, you can pick it up on your way back from work. You can send it then. What do you think?

Jenna: If it won't send at Walmart, it won't send at Western Union.

Eric: It will okay. Both are different transfers.

Jenna: Okay. I am not sure what time I will get out tonight.

Eric: Babe, you have to try your best.

Jenna: I may be in the field today with my new manager.

Eric: You know how important this is.

Jenna: I will try my best, but the money isn't going to be enough. And now we have to start paying for that before we can get you

out. There is always going to be something more to do. I am spending money that I really don't have to send.
Eric: I told you to send more money right NOW!

When he started to get angry, Jenna did tell Walmart that she never met this person that she was giving money to for eight months. She had called a lawyer two days before.

Jenna: I don't have more money to send.
Eric: You are getting me angry with your words. I just told you they could not pick up the $70 you sent, and you are saying something else. Listen, you can go take your money back. Don't send it to them. Enough with all the insults to my face.
Jenna: I am just saying that it has always been this way. Once we start paying, then we have to pay more for something else. I am not insulting you.
Eric: I told you there would be no more money. Didn't I tell you that? All we have to do is pay the money. I ask you to pay. That is all. Why are you saying all these things to me? Is it because I am in a situation like this? I hope you are doing okay.
Jenna: Yes, I am trying to upload stuff on the computer.
Eric: Okay. When will you be able to go to Walmart?
Jenna: No, not yet.
Eric: Okay, babe. What time are you going to be off from work?
Jenna: Capital One has not received their payment yet. I'm not sure what the holdup is. Let me check my text messages. They are having me take the. MoneyGram is looking into this and making sure everything is on the up and up. They will not have me send anything to you because right now, they think it is a scam.
Eric: Go to Western Union and send it!
Jenna: I can't go to Western Union because they wanted to have people talk to me the last time I went. I am so sorry I am cut off. I don't want to get in any kind of trouble, and I am not sure what this is all about. What is your address?
Eric: Babe, get an iTunes card.
Jenna: HUH?

Eric: You are going to scratch the iTunes card, take a photo of it, and
    send it to me here!
Jenna: Why an iTunes card?
Eric: Do IT!
Jenna: How is that going to help you? Excuse me? Do it?

This is where Jenna had enough. She went into Walmart, and
when they asked if she knew the person that she was sending money
to, she said, "*No*, I don't. I thought I knew him, and I thought he
could be trusted. But I have never met him or heard him. I have only
texted him." The people on the other line asked her for his name,
and Jenna said, "He calls himself Eric." However, she knew this was
not him because she had also called a lawyer, and he asked her to call
the FBI and let them know as well. The lawyer told Jenna that she
was being catfished. This is what they called it, and she played along
with him because in her heart, Jenna wanted to believe that they
had it wrong. She put the picture that he gave her into a database
called Social Catfish, and what came up was three hits and eighty-six
pictures.

After Eric told Jenna to do it and get an iTunes card, she knew
this was all a hoax and that she had been scammed by one of the best.
She cried profusely over him way too many times, then she stood in
her power and told the truth: "I have never spoken to this man or saw
him in person, only in a picture, and I don't know him."

Eric: Just do what I ask you, okay? Have you gotten it?
Jenna: I couldn't get it. They have a disclaimer now that says scam-
    mers are getting people to get iTunes gift cards. I don't know
    what you are into, but I don't want to be a part of it!
Eric: Oh, I see. Don't worry about it. Since you believe in them, you
    can go ahead. Bye. I know you will always come up with stories
    because you are I ga now. Bye.
Jenna: Bye.
Eric: I wish you the best.
Jenna: I wish you the best as well. I fell in love with you. While I was
    helping you, I prayed that you would do something good with

the money that I gave to you. You will be in my heart and mind. I wish you the best life has to offer.

September 24, 2019

Eric: That is not love. And as for your money, it will be returned to you soon, I promise. I know the total amount.
Jenna: Yes, it is. I am detaching with love, and someday you will see that.
Eric: I have your account details, so it will be transferred to you when I make my way out of here. I know you will always let me down. I know that already.
Jenna: My hands are tied right now. I have not let you down. I have been helping you as much as I could. You are a very smart man in the army. I will continue to pray for both of you. I need to work on getting myself out of the house I have been in. I could have been out of here already. I need to help my family and myself now. I have given you all I could. If you feel let down, that is all on you.

September 26, 2018

Eric: Thank you.
Jenna: I am checking on you because I still care about you.
Eric: No, you don't, but thanks. I really appreciate it.

September 29, 2018

I mistakenly hit the Call button on Hangouts and called him, ugh.

Eric: Why are you ringing me?
Jenna: I butt-dialed you by mistake, sorry.
Eric: Okay.
Jenna: Have a good weekend.

Eric: There's no need for that. Stop pretending like you care when both of us know you don't. Bye.

Jenna: I am moving out in October. My friend Debbie's mother passed away, and I was with her and her sister the whole night.

Jenna: It is caring, and I will not reach out again. You are acting like a spoiled brat. I think I just dodged a bullet. Have a nice life.

Eric: Thanks. Have a nice life. Bye.

Eric: You said I was a spoiled brat. Why you sending me a link to watch? The time will come where you will regret all you say to me. I wish you the best in life.

Eric: God is the greatest, not humans. I will stay in the war zone for one more year. If I make it out of here alive, I will send you back all your money.

Jenna: What they do is send a check to you, and after you cash it, a couple of days later, they take it out of the bank. And you owe all that money to your bank.

Jenna: I have nothing to go on. You have not opened up as why you need all this money. My hands are tied in getting the money to you. Yes, maybe someday you will open up and explain all that went to me, but right now all I can do for you is pray that you make it out alive and for Jerry's safety.

Eric: No, you don't have to pray for Jerry. You can pray for yourself. Like I told you, I will get you back your money. I don't need you to think the money is free. It will get to you. I have received a lot of insults from you. God knows why. Maybe you are more than what I am seeing.

October 1, 2019

Jenna: That is okay. I am still in love with you, and I am happy I could help you as much as I could. My heart knows how it feels. My head may still be figuring things out, but I can't imagine finding another man that makes me feel like you did. I am going to work on what I can here. It makes me sick to my stomach that I have lost your love.

Eric: You betrayed me, Jenna. You want ahead and called me names.

Jenna: There is nothing I can say to make it better. I told the truth as I know it.

Eric: The reason I told you to buy the iTunes card is because Jerry can get some money from it.

Jenna: 😥😥😥 [I was crying on the inside. I couldn't cry on the outside because no one knew what I was going through.]

Eric: That is the only way right now, but all you could do is shout out at me. Are you okay with the way you are treating the boy when you know he has a heart problem?

Jenna: No, I am not. And no, I did not know he had a heart problem. You never told me that. 😥😥😥 You told me Whitney and Jerry were sick. You never said it was his heart.

Jenna: 😥😥😥 It was his heart? Did he pass?

Eric: He's still in pain. I am still trying to work out his papers so that he can fly back to the States.

Jenna: [Now Jenna was crying profusely.] 😥😥😥

Eric: The $70 was for him to get some items before you disappointed him.

Jenna: 😥😥😥 [This is what they do. They play with your emotions and try to make you feel guilty. It has been way over a year since he started to text Jenna, and she has heard nothing from him at all.]

Eric: 😥😥😥

Jenna: I will love you whether you decide to go into another union or talk to me. That is what unconditional love is. Have you ever had anyone love you for you, without expectations? I may not have the money you need or the way to get the money once I do have it. That doesn't mean I turned the love off.

Jenna: I feel for you and this connection. I will be here when you need me. I am not like other women that only love you for what you can give them. I have been waiting for a love like this all my life. I have no conditions. I speak my truth as I know it even if it breaks my heart and soul.

Jenna: I just got a vision. I manifested this through the law of attraction. I wrote down on paper fifty-five times for five days. I should have been more specific on how to help you out.

Jenna: "Money comes to me in avalanches of abundance, and I will receive it and am able to help Eric out." I wrote that fifty-five times for five days.

Eric: Love endures all pain.

Jenna: 😥😥😥

The clock read 5:55, and the number 555 means change.

Eric: Okay. I have been in pain this period. I decided not to tell you anything that is going on with me. You always use it against me, so it is best to keep it to myself.

Jenna: 😥😥😥

Eric: I hope you are doing okay. I pray God will protect you in all you do in life.

Jenna: I feel the same for you. I have the car company coming to take my car right now. I have to leave.

Eric: I am sorry about that.

Jenna: I feel the same for you. My heart hurts.

Eric: I know it is all my fault about the company. I told them to send you back your money and let me lose my box, but they said that the money had been used for the document.

Jenna: It is okay. I will figure it out. I am moving out of Dan's house at the end of the month. My friend Debbie has asked us to move in with her.

Eric: Moving to where?

Jenna: I'm still in New Hampshire with my friend Debbie.

Eric: Okay. What about your new job?

Jenna: I am still here. That won't change.

Eric: Okay.

Jenna: How are you doing?

Eric: I am doing okay even when I am not.

Jenna: That is how I feel.

Eric: God will make a way.

Jenna: I am sorry I caused you pain and heartache. Yes, I believe in God.

Eric: Don't worry. It makes me stronger.

Jenna: I do love you still very much.

Eric: It hurt me bad that you turned me into your enemy. I know things are not better over there with you.

Jenna: My enemy?

Eric: Yes, because if you were not, you wouldn't have listened to other people.

Jenna: I answered the questions that the authorities asked me to answer.

Eric: I even told you to go to Western Union, and you refused.

Jenna: I told them I didn't know you.

Eric: Are the authorities more important than me?

Jenna: Western Union would have asked me as well.

Eric: You could have told them you were sending it to your friend to pay the bills.

Jenna: No, you are important to me, but I am a licensed agent and cannot do what you want me to do now that I know that it is illegal.

Eric: It's okay. We don't have to argue about it.

Jenna: I didn't want to lie. They asked if I have ever seen you, and I said I have seen pictures.

Eric: You were the one who did wrong. You could have told them yes.

Jenna: And you have seen pictures of me, and I am real.

Eric: You could have said yes to prevent so many questions. Do you still have the $70 with you? You are not talking.

Jenna: They caught me off guard. I had to use the $70 for gas money this week.

Eric: When are you going to receive your salary?

Jenna: I have no idea.

Eric: Are you are working with them? You should have known by now.

Jenna: It is commission, and I haven't started selling the product yet.

Eric: Okay.

October 3, 2018

Jenna: I wish things were different between us. I have ruined everything and have been sick to my stomach.

Eric: I'm sorry about that, okay?

Jenna: I didn't do wrong. I answered honestly. We have never seen each other, and I have only seen pictures of you. You have seen pictures of me. I am real. They asked if I ever heard your voice. I said no and that we knew each other and texted each other online. And I told them I have only known you for six months.

October 7, 2018

Jenna: I'm just checking on you. I hope you are okay.

Eric: Yeah. I hope you are doing okay over there.

Jenna: I am okay.

Jenna sent some fall foliage pictures as she was taking a walk on the rail trail.

Eric: Oh, that is nice.

October 8, 2018

Jenna: Yes, I went for a walk and took pictures of the leaves.

Jenna: I woke up early and thought of how I used to take walks and send you pictures before, when we were together. It made me think of you. I am glad you are doing well with your new, special love. I wish things could have been different. I'm just checking to see how you are doing.

Eric: I never had another lover. The only woman I had betrayed me because of money. I could not betray anyone because of money.

Jenna: I told my truth after giving myself to you over and over and over again. As the authorities told me, I really don't have any idea what you are using the money for. It could be drugs, sex trafficking, guns, or parties. I have already given you every bit of money that I have to give. I have nothing left, even for me, and you are making me feel guilty for giving you everything I had to give. Did I betray you? I helped you for months. I worried

about you for months. Who betrayed who here? I could say the
same thing about you.

Jenna: Every time I paid a certain amount, you would need more,
like $70, $1,000, $2,800, $4,800, $3,200, etc.

Jenna: Yes, I finally told the authorities the truth. If our love was
strong enough, it wouldn't have fallen apart. I have played my
part in your journey. I have helped you along your path. I feel
bad about telling the truth and hurting you and Jerry, but it
needed to come out. And I cannot change what happened.

Jenna: I can only learn from the lesson, ask for forgiveness, and move
on with my life the best that I can.

Eric: God bless you always. Know that your heart is with me in every-
thing even though I don't have access to my money. I always
pray for protection and a good-paying job for you. I wish you a
good morning. Let your boss be kind to you today.

Jenna: I am sorry I hurt you. That was not my intention. I love you,
and you will always have a piece of my heart. My wish for you is
that you will get out of wherever you are and that you will find
comfort in knowing that you found love with someone and will
do so again.

Jenna: I know it will not be with me, and as much as it is tearing me
apart, I have to trust in God and his infinite wisdom. I can't
change the past. I can only change myself and how I react in
situations. I never meant to bring you harm.

Eric: May God be with you and all you do in life.

Jenna: You as well. May God protect you and your family in all you
do.

Eric: Thank you. Your money will be given back to you. Don't worry.

Jenna: Just concentrate on getting out of there first. I will worry
about myself. I worry about you and want you to be happy.

Eric: How will I be when nobody cares about me?

Jenna: I care. I just don't have money to get you out, and I can't send
money to you.

Eric: You could deposit it in an account. They will give me an account
you can send it through.

October 10, 2018

Jenna: When I get a good check, I can still do that, but right now I am still learning and am not getting paid while I learn.

Jenna: We should have done that before with the accounts and not gone to Western Union and Walmart. [Don't do this. They give you a check to put into the bank, and when you go to use the money, the money is not there. You will owe the amount that they gave to you.]

Eric: Okay. When are you going to get your check?

Jenna: I don't know. I am still at the end of my training. Open enrollment for under sixty-five starts November 1. I missed the Medicare open enrollment. There was not enough time to teach me that. I haven't been appointed to that yet.

Eric: Okay.

Jenna sent a "manifestation of money" YouTube video.

Eric: Thank you.

Jenna: 🙏

Jenna: You will manifest in twenty-four hours or less.

Eric: Thank you, babe.

Jenna: You are welcome.

Eric: In this crazy world full of change. there is one thing of which I am certain, one thing that does not change. Good morning.

Jenna: What would that be?

Eric: It's my love for you even when you keep betraying me.

Jenna: How do I keep betraying you?

Eric: You know what I mean. You always change when it comes to helping me. You always come up with different excuses, and you are always listening to different people.

Jenna: Look, I am not blaming you. I know you needed the money I gave you for whatever reason. At this moment, I don't have any money to give to you. I haven't received a check. You are not here to text anymore. You try to catch me in things to show that I betrayed you. In my heart, I know it was you that betrayed me.

Eric: Oh, I see. I guess you have someone else.

Jenna: The man I fell in love with does not exist. He is not talking to me. When he does talk to me, it is in anger, and he feels that I betrayed him.

Jenna: I am talking to people. I told them I am still healing from a love that I thought would be forever. We did have an argument, but we both are still talking. But it's not like before. Guys will tell me not to live in the past and go to the future, but I can't because I am still in love with you, whoever you are.

Eric: You know I love you so much, and the most important thing is love and trust.

Jenna: I love you so much, but I don't know what to do with this whole situation.

Eric: You have to face your fear. No relationship is purely sunshine. We were supposed to work as a team, not argue or fight.

Jenna: I love you. I trust what you are telling me is real, but I don't know how to fix it. I can't help it if men talk to me. I don't go out looking for them. I tell them straight up that I am in love with someone.

Eric: Don't tell them your name. Keep this a secret between both of us, okay? What are you doing at the moment?

Jenna: I'm feeding Milo. Why is everything so secretive?

Eric: Honey, don't forget that I am working for the United Nations.

Jenna: Other guys say they are working with the United Nations as well. I had a guy call me on the phone last night, and he sounded Italian. He has a daughter and is nice, but he is not you. [Jenna knew this was another scammer, but she did not tell Eric this. In her heart, she wanted to believe that this was all a mistake and that Eric would come and prove to her that he was a real person, not someone who made up this fabricated plot to get as much money out of her as possible.]

* * * * *

I put this other scammer's picture in socialcatfish.com, and it came up with several hits. I didn't have the heart to put Eric's picture that he gave me into the site, but I eventually did. And he came up with three different hits of scamming people. Later in my group, I saw another woman who posted the same picture he sent to me to see if he was real, and I told her my story and said to not give him a dime! He is not real.

I did help one person so far but hope to let this book go through everyone else who is in this situation right now. I have since learned that sometimes the scammer will want you to come and take care of their children, and when you go there, you will be taken in a van and brought overseas to a sex trafficking group or drug trafficking group. These people prey on your vulnerability, and they make you slaves to them, as our ancestors made them slaves a long time ago. Even though we had nothing to do with our ancestors' horrid behavior, they feel it is their right to get us back for us to pay karma for what our forefathers did in the past.

Eric wanted me to go and sign for a box that he had. If I did that, I would have brought the FBI in to make sure this was legitimate. However, it never got that far. Thank you, God.

I have seen where a woman signed a document at the airport, and the person had drugs lined in the bag. She got arrested and is in jail for the rest of her life because she trusted someone and fell in love. We didn't stay on long. He just wanted to show me it was real.

* * * * *

Eric: So you have been chatting with other guys?

No, Jenna was chatting with guys that were like him so she could catch their asses before they could do what Eric did to her.])

Jenna: Last night I talked to someone. Yes, for five minutes, maybe. I told him I was still in love with you. I will gladly give them all up, but I don't want to be waiting here for days, months, or years. You and I haven't even had any kind of talking through the phone after six months of being together. The man asked if I was still in touch with you, and I said yes but that it isn't like

it was before. If you don't want me to talk to them, then you
at least need to start talking to me and letting me know what is
going on.

Eric: You can keep talking to them since that will make you happy.

Jenna: It doesn't make me happy. None of this makes me happy. I get
texts from you of just one or two words, and I am supposed to
save myself for you?

Eric: Yes, because you made a statement.

Jenna: We used to text every day. You said I betrayed you, and I spoke
my truth. I don't go around telling everyone that you left me
penniless and that I had to go to my friend's house and hide my
car so they wouldn't take it. I had to ask another friend if she
could pay for one car payment so they wouldn't take my car,
which I still owe her for. I can't sell some insurance products
because my credit is bad, and I don't have money to make it
better. I haven't blamed you even though I could have paid off
all that with the money I gave to you.

Jenna: I can't sleep at night, worrying about when I will get my next
check, and all you do is keep saying that I betrayed you.

Jenna: I don't see how any of this is going to get better.

Eric: I want you to know that I love you, and I will never forget all
that you have done.

Jenna: I want you to know I love you as well.

Eric: I just want to leave here and fulfill all that I promised you. I will
never betray your love for me.

Jenna: I will never forget the passion you showed me.

Eric: I don't go around chatting with people. I am honest and 100
percent faithful.

Jenna: No, but you blame me for betraying you and don't talk to me
for days, and I am supposed to sit here, twiddle my thumbs,
and wait for a man who may or may not get in touch with me?

Eric: Okay. I hope you are doing okay.

Jenna: It is good. I did a quote for someone and scheduled to go and
see them. I talked to sixty-two people today.

Eric: Okay. Have you eaten?

Jenna: No, how about you?

Eric: Same here. How was work today?

Jenna: It was good. I got a 92 on my mock exam.

October 13, 2018

Jenna: I just got up. It is 2:46 a.m.

Eric: Okay, babe. You have been working the whole day, so you need some rest.

Jenna: I fell asleep again, and now I am up at 4:41 a.m.

Eric: Okay, babe. What are your plans in the morning?

Jenna: I will take a walk, call people, and schedule appointments with them.

Eric: Okay.

Jenna: What are your plans?

Eric: I don't have plans now.

Jenna: Why?

Eric: I am tired of everything.

Jenna: What is going on? Try to get yourself on a higher vibration. Try this YouTube meditation video.

Eric: Thanks, babe.

Jenna: You are welcome. I hope it helps.

Eric: I am depressed.

Jenna: It is okay to feel sad at times. Let the feelings come, but know you will get stronger. You are a strong and resilient man. Acknowledge the depression. Ask why it is here. What do you have to learn from it? Take a bath. Use sea salt to get rid of the negative energy.

Eric: Thank you, babe. You remain the best.

Jenna: You are welcome, my king. I'm just checking on you to see how you are doing.

Eric: Thank you for your love and support.

Jenna: You are welcome.

Eric: What are you doing at the moment?

Jenna: I'm in line at Dunkin' Donuts, getting coffee. I hope you are feeling a little better. I had some change in my purse. It was enough to get a large coffee.

Eric: I'm getting better a little. How is the weather over there?
Jenna: It is cold, wet, and rainy. No walk for me. How is the weather there?
Eric: Can't you borrow some money from her?
Jenna: No, she just bought a condo, and I wouldn't ask her to do that. She is strapped. I feel bad enough for asking her to make a car payment for me.

October 13, 2018
4:42 p.m.

Jenna: So are you feeling better? 10 just dyed my hair 6.99. My son paid for the box of color. I am okay. I feel like I am getting a cold. Hopefully, it is an allergy. I was just watching my nephews. My son is with me.
Eric: Okay, babe. How is your son?
Jenna: He is good.
Eric: It's good to hear that.
Jenna: Yeah. How are you feeling now?
Eric: Never ever change because I love you the way you are.
Eric: Good morning.

Eric sent a picture of a coffee cup.

Jenna: Good morning. I'm just checking on you and seeing how you are doing.
Eric: Thank you, babe. Love makes us overcome the greatest and the most challenging obstacles. It shows us what it means to love someone unconditionally and care for their happiness as if it is our own. Love may sometimes make us do things that are a little bit crazy and stupid. But most of the time, love inspires us greatly. Good morning, babe.
Jenna: Good morning to you. I love the coffee cup with a musical note on it.
Eric: Thanks, babe. I miss you.
Jenna: I miss you too. I'm trying to get over a cold.

Eric: You are all that matters to me. My love for you will last eter-
nally. Good morning, babe.
Jenna: Good morning. XOXO
Eric: How was your night, babe?
Jenna: Good, and yours?
Eric: Splendid. What are you doing at the moment?
Jenna: Waking up from sleeping.
Eric: What are your plans today?
Jenna: I am working, and you?
Eric: I am off from work.
Jenna: Is that good or bad?
Eric: Good.

October 17, 2018

Eric: How was your night?
Jenna: It was good. How was yours?
Eric: I am doing okay. Thanks for asking. How is work?
Jenna: It is okay. There are a lot more people coming in, and it is
busy. How is yours?
Eric: Mine is okay.
Jenna: That is good. What are you doing now?
Eric: I am in my duty post now. I hope you are okay, babe. I pray
everything will be okay with you. I am worried about you, and
may God be with you in all you do.
Jenna: Sorry. My phone wasn't working. I had to get a new one, and
I couldn't figure out how to get Hangouts on my new phone.
Jenna: I hope you are okay.
Eric: Sorry about that.
Jenna: No worries, I figured it out. I miss you.
Eric: I miss you too. I hope you are taking very good care of yourself.
Jenna: I am. How about you?
Eric: I am fine.
Jenna: Good. I am sorry about the other two guys I was texting and
talking about. I am no longer talking to them. I don't want to

spoil what we have together. You are very special to me, some-
one I never want to forget.

Jenna: Next weekend, I am moving.

Eric: Okay, honey. I am glad you have someplace good to stay before
I get home.

Jenna: Me too. When will you be home, love? Have they told you?

Eric: Babe, not yet. That is the reason I told you the only solution,
and you have not done anything about it yet.

Jenna: It is not that I haven't done anything. It is that I can't right
now. Hopefully, soon I will start making money, love.

Eric: Babe, can you raise $1,000 by next week so they can start the
processing?

Jenna: I am not sure. Love, I will try my best. Do you only have
$1,000 left?

Eric: Okay, babe. Thank you. Where are you at the moment?

Jenna: I was at work. My computer was running slow, so I came
home to call people.

Eric: Okay, babe.

Jenna: I really miss you. I wish you were closer. I would drive to pick
you up.

Eric: I miss you too, honey. Soon you are going to pick me up at the
airport.

Jenna: I will be waiting for that day. It has been a long time coming.
The Manchester airport is near my house.

Eric: Yes, babe. You told me that. Babe, please, you have to try your
best next week, okay?

Jenna: Okay.

Eric: Have you eaten, babe?

Jenna: I ate just popcorn. How about you?

Eric: Nothing, babe. It is late over here.

Jenna: It is 5:25 p.m. You are probably sleeping. I hope I don't wake
you up. I have been seeing 888.

Jenna sent Eric Robert Zink's 888 video on YouTube.

Eric: What number is that, babe? You mean 888?
Jenna: Yes, I am seeing it all over the place and 999.

October 20, 2018

Jenna: I hope you have a good day today. I am going to Connecticut today with my friend Debbie to get some stuff from her house and move it to her condo. She has two houses. Ugh, I still have a cold and am not feeling very good.
Eric: I understand, babe. Please look after yourself, okay?
Jenna: Okay. Please look after yourself as well. I love you.
Eric: I love you too. Please stay safe.
Jenna: I will. Debbie is driving.
Eric: Okay, babe.
Jenna: How are you doing, my king?
Eric: I am doing okay, my queen, and you?
Jenna: I am sorry I fell asleep. I have been fighting off a cold.
Eric: I understand you perfectly, honey. You have to rest, okay?

October 21, 2018

Jenna: Yeah, I can't believe I slept until 11:30 a.m. I never do that.
Eric: You have not gotten time to rest very well. So you need this.
Jenna: No, I haven't. Everyone is going in and out, being noisy, and playing loud music on their phones. And sleeping in the living room, on a recliner, doesn't help. I can't wait to get out of the house.
Eric: Have you taken breakfast?
Jenna: I am just making tea, and have you had something to eat? I really miss texting you.
Eric: I've had nothing to eat yet. I miss you more. I miss the way we used to play and chat.
Jenna: Yeah, I miss that too. You need to eat something.
Eric: Yes, will do, okay? How is your friend doing, babe? Have you moved to her place?

Jenna: She is doing well. No, not yet. This weekend we went to her house to bring things to her condo.

Eric: Okay.

Jenna: Somewhere along the many texts we have shared, I started to fall in love with you. I don't know when it happened. I just know I did. Those chiseled cheekbones and that beautiful stare in your eyes melted my soul. [Jenna fell in love with a picture that this person sent to her. She believed that this was the man that she was texting with for eight months. All she knows now is that the picture was not the man that she thought she was talking to.]

Eric: You rule my world, babe, and you know that.

Jenna: Oh my gosh, I am horrible with this texting.

Eric: Smile. You deserve the best.

Jenna: I never get the words right. I have the best. That is you.

Eric: Same. Babe, what are you doing?

Jenna: I'm talking with Debbie.

Eric: Babe, I want you to try your best. Remember what we discussed a few days back?

Jenna: Yes, I remember.

Eric: Thank you, babe.

Jenna: I took some SUDAFED. I am feeling better. I think this was an allergy. I can't wait to come and pick you up at the airport.

Eric: Yes, babe. I love you more. I always want you to know that.

Jenna: I love you so much.

Eric: Hi, babe. How are you doing?

Jenna: Hi. How are you?

Eric: I am fine, honey. How is work going?

Jenna: Awww, I am good. I'm making appointments. I am moving to Merrimack, New Hampshire.

Eric: There may be many beautiful women but none as beautiful as you. The day you entered my life, my whole world was filled with happiness. You always stood by my side, and now I promise you that I will shower you with all my love and time. Good morning, my beautiful wife. [He called Jenna his wife when he wanted to butter her up and get her to give him more money.

She was never married to him, but she did fall in love with the way he treated her.]

Jenna: Good morning, my handsome husband. How was your night? How is your day going?

Eric: My day is okay, babe. Thank you. What about you?

Jenna: I am waking up to the printer and people talking in the living room, where I was sleeping.

Eric: Okay, honey. Do we have any good news?

* * * * *

Eric was asking about the company he had his box at. He had me send an email asking if we could extend the date to help get the money for Eric's box. The plan he had was for me to pay for the box so he could get out of the war zone. This was all an intricate scam. If I had signed for his box, I could have gone to prison. The thing they do is get the person to trust them enough to sign for their box, and when you sign for that box, then you are responsible for the consequences. The box usually has drugs or weapons in it, not money, that is theirs; and when you take ownership of this box, you can go to jail for that. I wouldn't have let it get to that point. I would have called the FBI and had someone come with me just in case. I have watched TV shows on this, and they believe this is our karma for our ancestors, who made them slaves. We are paying for our ancestors' sins.

* * * * *

Jenna: No. They called me, but the company hasn't given them a decision yet. December 21 is when they will come back with a decision. They may call sooner.

Eric: When do you think they will call?

Jenna: I don't know. Say your prayers Eric. [At this point, Jenna had called a lawyer and knew that the person in the picture was not the person she was texting for eight months.]

It was also then that she found out that the term for this was *catfishing*. She knew that Eric was not really the Eric she thought she had been talking to. She was devastated. (Yes, it was me that went through this, but talking in the third person makes it a little better for me to get through this.) The lawyer told her that she should call the FBI and tell them what she told him, which she did. Jenna cried so hard, knowing what this person did to her. She told the FBI agent that the person texted her every day and that it was almost worth giving the money to him because he treated her like a queen. The FBI agent said they could never get the money back because they were on a different continent. Jenna was told that her money was probably used for drugs, weapons, parties, or sex trafficking. The money did not go to his son's heart condition or his box.

* * * * *

I decided to write this book for all the women and the men that have gone through this or are going through this now. The man in the picture that was sent to me was a very handsome man. This handsome man had no idea his picture was on the Internet. I have learned that he was a decorated war hero.

When this book is finished, I will block him forever. I can no longer get to all my texts on Hangouts.

I am not sure how he did it, but I can't see any of our texts. The only way I could write this book is because I started writing everything down. There are months that are not here because I cannot get to my texts, and my notebooks are not all here because I have moved so many times this year.

* * * * *

Eric: I am a God-fearing man, and I trust God.
Jenna: Yes, you are. When you pray, things come to fruition.
Jenna: I am getting ready to go to work. I'm putting makeup on. What are you doing?
Eric: I am still doing paperwork.

Jenna: Wow, you do so much paperwork. Good for you for getting it done.
Eric: Yes, babe.

October 23, 2018

Eric: Hi, babe. How are you doing today?
Jenna: Hi. How are you?
Eric: I'm fine, and you? For the past few days, you did not say anything to me. I guess it is because of what I have asked of you, right?

He wanted Jenna to go to Walmart to get money orders from other people and send them to his friend Whitney. That was when she called a lawyer because she couldn't figure it out why he would want her to send the money and why the women wouldn't just send the money themselves. It didn't feel right to Jenna. It was one thing when she was sending her own money, but when he started sending her money orders, she called and spoke to the FBI.

* * * * *

It has been humbling for me. I have lost everything, even all of my savings.

I have lost my car, but I would like to say thanks to my friends. They sold their car to me for $1. I have put money into it to keep it on the road, and I pray that I get to pay them more money. I have been blessed with friends. I've been helping some of the friends I have paid back, and there are some I still need to pay back.

* * * * *

Jenna: No, I have been busy. I don't have the money. I have made $400 in nine weeks. I am trying to keep my car and concentrate on making money and helping my roommate move.
Eric: Okay.

October 27, 2018

Jenna: How are you doing?
Eric: I am doing okay. How are you doing?
Jenna: I am stressed from moving and being pulled in three different directions.
Eric: Oh, okay.

November 5, 2018
9:33 p.m.

Jenna: Are you okay? I haven't heard from you. I hope you are doing okay.

November 6, 2018

Eric: Is there any need to ask? You found yourself someone else. So I don't see any reason you need to ask.
Jenna: What are you talking about?
Eric: Reread my message.
Jenna: I haven't found anyone else. I am working and moving.

November 6, 2018

Eric: I am not important to you, and that is one of the reasons.
Jenna: I am trying to get my feet back on the ground from being stripped of all of my money. I am trying to pay for my car so they won't take it from me, and I am not important to you unless I am making a paycheck.
Eric: Oh, I see. That is what you think.
Jenna: Actions speak louder than words.
Eric: You can move on. Don't worry. Have a nice day.
Jenna: You too.
Eric: Thank you.
Jenna: I wish you the best life has to offer.

November 10, 2018

Jenna accidently pressed the Call button.

Eric: Did you call me?
Jenna: I'm sorry I pressed the Call button by mistake when I was listening to the songs you sent me. I hope I didn't wake you.

November 11, 2018

Eric: No, don't worry about that.
Jenna: I just had a guy call my phone and ask for an Eric. He sounded American. I didn't say anything, but you are the only Eric I know. Why would he think you were here with me? This is the guy's phone number.
Eric: Okay, I will try to find out.
Jenna: Okay. I just wanted to give you a heads-up.

Jenna was not giving him money, but she still had feelings for him. And she couldn't believe this was happening. She had no idea who the guy was. He asked for Eric, and she didn't say a thing. Then he hung up. It might be someone who had this number before. But the guy that everyone called for through Jenna's phone was named Steve, and he was a car salesman. This guy sounded older and asked if Eric was there.

Eric: Oh, okay. You can block his number, then.
Jenna: How do I block him? Oh, okay, I figured it out. I didn't notice that his number said. It's a scam, likely.
Eric: Oh, okay.

November 16, 2018

Jenna and Eric did not text each other again.

January 13, 2019
6:19 a.m.

Eric: Happy New Year.
Jenna: Happy New Year to you.
Eric: I hope you are doing okay.
Jenna: Yes, I have a roof over my head, food on the table, and heat.
    How are you?
Eric: I am doing okay. I don't need to complain.
Jenna: So are you out of the army? [She knew he wasn't in the army.]

May 14, 2019

Jenna accidently sent the letter *F* to Eric. She was writing a book, and she pressed the button by mistake.

June 12, 2019

Eric: Hi. How are you doing?
Jenna: Good, and you?

* * * * *

Eric saw I was on Hangouts. And I tried to copy and paste the conversations, but there was so much to copy that I couldn't get it all down on paper. So I hand wrote notebooks and notebooks of pages, and I have lost some of them.

* * * * *

Eric: I'm fine. It's been a long time. Where have you been all this
    time?

July 3, 2019

Eric: Baby, how are you doing today?

July 4, 2019

Eric: You read my messages but didn't reply.
Jenna: My car got repossessed because of me helping you. I am primarily living out of my car because of helping you. You didn't keep your promise of paying me back.
Jenna: Now I am in a financial bind.

July 5, 2019

Eric: Baby, why are you saying that I didn't keep my promise? I told you I am going to pay you back all the money when I am home with you. But you refuse to get me out of here. You value your money more than our love and happiness. You value your money more than my life. [They try to play on your emotions to make you feel guilty and like you are the one who has the problem.] Is that right to you? I would pay back all the money, but how? And you expect that I do that when I am still suffering? You know I don't have access to any of my properties when am still here, so how did I fail to keep my promise?
Jenna: I guess we are both out of luck, then.
Eric: I don't believe that, okay? We were almost there before you gave up on us. We should be together by now, baby.
Eric: But you choose to be alone and let me suffer and die here.

Jenna knew who this person was now. Because of Social Catfish, she knew this story was a made-up story and not real. She decided to call his bluff. This is what she said.

Jenna: Okay, where are you now? I know someone in the army that can help you in Iran.
Eric: Iran? Who is he? How well do you know him?
Jenna: He is someone who can help you. Just let me know what patrol you are in.
Eric: That does not answer my question. How well do you know him? Who is he to you?

Jenna didn't know anyone. She was trying to get information about his whereabouts. Jenna told him it was a high school buddy of hers. She also told him they couldn't exchange names because he knew the privacy rules. She totally called his bluff.

Jenna hasn't heard from Eric again.

Some days she prays that Eric is not suffering. She does have guilt of not being able to help a friend. She is no longer in love with a stranger she hopes and prays that this is really a scammer like everyone told her. She prays that Eric is in a safe place and not hurting anyone else and not scamming anyone else.

* * * * *

I did help one person that put his picture on a site, and on that site, I saw him and told her not to send him any money whatsoever because that man was not the man she was talking to. There is a link on Facebook to Social Catfish. You can upload a photo on your phone and then put it in Social Catfish to see if the photo has any hits.

For all of you in the same predicament, do not meet them—ever. They could be sex-trafficking. Before you send any money, make sure it is a person you already know. If not, do not send money to them.

I wrote this book because I didn't know about any of this going on, and if I did, I would have stopped paying a long time ago. I wasn't able to find all the months of texts that we had written to each other. My wish for all of you is to read this and take heart to what has happened to me so that the same thing will not happen to you.

On July 8, I had to move back to my parents' home. I had friends from Merrimack, Manchester, and Salem, New Hampshire, and family from Rockland and Holliston who have taken me in this year. I will be very grateful for all the people who have helped me on this tough, long, hard road.

I pray that if you are giving money to someone who you do not know, please stop and call a lawyer and the FBI. Do not give to someone who will never repay you and who will never ever meet you but wants to see you go to jail for your ancestors' sins. That is just not right.

Also on July 8, my roommate told me that her brother was moving in from the Dominican Republic with his three children and that I would have to move out. I walked for ten miles before I called my parents. My mother was not pleased about me moving back in because my sister doesn't like me and is living there. Her response to me was "Well, you have nowhere else to go, so you will have to come here." I am grateful for her taking me in, and I tried not to be a bother and stay out of everyone's way. But it was a challenge. I finally moved out at the end of September and am living with my cousin Sue and her family. I will be forever in their debt for taking me in and being the pillars that I needed to stand on my feet again.

Thank you for reading this all the way through, and I hope and pray that if you or anyone you know is in the same predicament, you will give them this book or tell them about Social Catfish.

ABOUT THE AUTHOR

 Wanda Stevens Reilly was raised in Quincy, Massachusetts, and moved to Rockland in 1972. In 1980, she graduated from Rockland High School. She was a makeup artist from '80 to '85 and went to the John Robert Powers modeling school in Boston in her twenties.

Wanda had her first child in 1990 and her second child in '92. She moved to Goffstown, New Hampshire, in 1992 and divorced in 2007. She was a medical coder for sixteen and a half years in Manchester, New Hampshire, and Nashua, New Hampshire. Wanda was a COC and a CPC. She also tried her hand at insurance, although she wasn't very good at it. They said she was too nice.

After the fiasco with the scammer and not having a huge amount of money with her, she moved to Tennessee in 2020. She met a very nice man in 2021 and is still with him today. She lives with him and his mother in Tennessee, and she thanks them very much for all the support that they've given her through these two years. The man is a very private person, so she won't mention him by name. But he knows who he is.